Learning Entrepreneurship Through Indigenous Knowledge

Henry M. Bwisa
&
Fredrick Muyia Nafukho

Nsemia

First Edition: July 2012

Edited by: Melecki Khayesi
Cover Design: Danielle Pitt
Layout Design: Kemunto Matunda

Published by Nsemia Inc. Publishers (www.nsemia.com); Oakville, Ontario, Canada

Note for Librarians: A cataloguing record for this book is available from Library and Archives Canada

ISBN: 978-1-926906-19-5 paperback

DEDICATIONS

To our parents and grandparents who introduced us to fairy tales

TABLE OF CONTENTS

ABOUT THE AUTHORS

Professor Henry M. Bwisa

Prof. Bwisa was born 58 years ago in the village of Lutonyi in Kimilili location of present-day Bungoma County. He went to Kimilili primary school before ending up at Friends School Kamusinga where he did both his O and A levels. In 1977 he received a government scholarship to study enterprise development in the then Soviet Union.

Prof. Bwisa has taught at primary, secondary, college and university levels. In 1992 he chaired a Jomo Kenyatta University of Agriculture and Technology Committee which institutionalized entrepreneurship education in Kenya making it the first university in the region to introduce entrepreneurship education at university level. He has served the country in various capacities including chairing the Kenya Invest Authority and is a member of several local and international bodies.

Prof. Bwisa has extensively researched in and published on entrepreneurship. His 2011 publication – Entrepreneurship theory and practice – a Kenyan perspective – is the first locally authored textbook of entrepreneurship in Kenya.

Professor Fredrick Muyia Nafukho, Ph.D.

Prof Nafukho is a professor of educational administration and human resource development and Head, Department of Educational Administration and Human Resource Development, College of Education and Human Development, Texas A&M University, USA. He attended Namulungu Primary School, St. Peters Mumias Boys High School, and Kwale High School. He obtained a bachelor of education degree in Business Studies and Economics, and a Masters degree in Economics of Education, both from Kenyatta University, Kenya. He obtained his PhD in Human Resource Development from Louisiana State University where he was a Fulbright Scholar. He is author of *Foundations of Adult Education in Africa (2005)* and *Management of Adult Education Organizations in Africa (2011).*

Dr. Nafukho has also designed and successfully delivered online courses. He has written extensively on the need for Information and Communication Technology policies for African countries, entrepreneurship and youth unemployment in Africa, and emotional intelligence and leadership development. He has served as a consultant with the UNDP, WHO and UNESCO and has facilitated training workshops on Emotional Intelligence and Leadership Development. He served as a lead consultant for 15 Southern African Development Community (SADC) on a Four Sector Study on Open and Distance Learning Research Project. Prof. Nafukho has also written extensively on performance improvement, the Market Model of Financing Universities in Africa, the University Loan Policies in Africa and US, international HRD, e-learning and training and development and has served as an external examiner to University of Cape Town, South Africa, Catholic University of Eastern Africa, Egerton University, The University of Eastern Africa, Baraton, The University of the North-West at Mafeking and University of Nairobi among others. His research interest include adult learning, organizational learning and performance improvement, enterprise development, evaluation in organizations, investment in human capital development, national and international human resource development.

FOREWORD

An African proverb that has great meaning for me is that "When a village elder dies, the village loses a library."

The authors have documented well the wisdom contained in the spoken words, proverbs and sayings of these elders that have served to guide generations of Africans in their daily actions and activities.

The authors have taken the spoken words of African elders, as well as their own experiences, and have presented this knowledge regarding entrepreneurship in written form.

Most of us act in entrepreneurial ways in our personal life, family life, community activities, in our jobs and being self-employed. The concepts presented in this book will help young people be more entrepreneurial in all aspects of their lives.

Bob Nelson, Ph.D
Senior Scholar in Residence & Senior Advisor
Academy for Entrepreneurial Leadership
University of Illinois at Urbana, Champaign
Illinois; USA

PART ONE

Introduction on Entrepreneurship and How to Use the Book

When planning for a year, plant rice. When planning for a decade plant trees. When planning for life, train and educate people. (Chinese proverb).

CHAPTER ONE

INTRODUCTION

This book is meant to stimulate entrepreneurial attitudes and behaviour among young readers. It has been noted in the literature that fairy tales have been used successfully to teach economics to children, as noted, "Many adults have a hard time fully understanding the complexities of economics and so teaching the subject to elementary-school students might seem impossible. But believe it or not, fairy tales effectively demonstrate basic economic principles and depict a variety of economic experiences in a way children can truly understand" (Weldon-Lassiter, 2002, p. 1). Since entrepreneurship and economics can be likened to cousins the same can be said about the teaching of entrepreneurship to children.

In our long teaching careers, we have met a number of entrepreneurs who did point to us that they had a parent or close relative or family friend who ran their own businesses. This has made us to raise the question - What happens to kids who live in many impoverished African communities where entrepreneurial business opportunities are rare, and parents are unemployed, underemployed, or simply struggling to get by? This is one of the objectives of this book - it seeks to demonstrate to all children that entrepreneurial culture can be learned at a young age from family members, family friends or by listening to stories told at the dinner table or evening fireplace. Our experiences, having grown up with our grandparents in rural Kenya who used to tell us many fairy tales is that children normally identify with the characters in the tales and some even extend themselves by engaging their imaginations in role-playing the characters. We strongly believe that using fairy tales and stories based on Indigenous Knowledge (IK) is a powerful means of developing an entrepreneurial culture among children. In this book, an entrepreneurial characteristic and therefore principle is paired with one or more fairy tales or stories. With practice, educators and parents and even kids themselves will begin to see how one tale/story can be used to highlight more than one entrepreneurship characteristic.

Entrepreneurial attitudes gained through this book will be seedbeds that will help children contribute to families, organizations, communities and ultimately the nation as they learn to turn challenges and opportunities into cultural, social, environmental, or financial wealth. Indeed research shows that entrepreneurship is best learned at a young age (Nafukho, 1998). Children who are taught about entrepreneurship are more likely to start their own businesses and more likely to succeed with these businesses.

The book is intended primarily for parents and teachers/trainers alike to use the tales to inculcate the entrepreneurial culture among children. The other audiences who will immensely benefit from the tales include the children themselves who can read the tales as a way of cultivating a career in entrepreneurship and using African Indigenous Knowledge to address one of the core issues facing the continent – wealth creation.

WHY USE THIS BOOK?

The search for appropriate books to use in addressing complex societal problems such as unemployment, underemployment, wealth creation, environmental degradation, poverty alleviation, and business failures, still remains unresolved. We need books that emphasize the need to embrace values of the indigenous knowledge systems of various peoples world over. While several books have been written or are being written on entrepreneurship and wealth creation in Africa, the challenge to complement these books is more felt now than ever before. We see a major gap in some inspiring indigenous knowledge systems such as the African folktales and proverbs which are mainly oral in nature but full of wisdom and knowledge that can be captured to address contemporary societal problems. There has been an increasing interest in the role culture plays in determining entrepreneurial success and in harnessing existing opportunities. Every society since the beginning of time has developed its own mechanisms and institutions for passing on pertinent knowledge and wisdom from one generation to the next through social learning (Bandura, 1977). With the advent of technology this process is even made more meaningful. In the case of Africa for instance, there has been a growing interest in the use of proverbs and folk tales as a teaching strategy. This book therefore uses folktales to teach entrepreneurship among children and the youths to inculcate the entrepreneurial culture. The book will serve not only as a resource material for teachers, educators, parents, students, workers, policy makers, and business leaders in Africa, but should create an opportunity for Africans and people world over to read about the African Indigenous Knowledge Systems rarely captured in written form.

This book is meant for a very wide readership for there is no single book of its kind that exists so far. Ideally, it is to be a school-level textbook for all school children, teachers and parents. It also targets government officials concerned with wealth creation policies, and Non-governmental executives and workers. It is meant for those engaged in NGO-related development issues and workplace learning adults. It is thus meant for both specialist professional readers and general readers. It will also be relevant to individuals with interest in entrepreneurship with multidisciplinary focus such as indigenous knowledge systems, history, science, technology, sociology, psychology, philosophy, religion and anthropology, and fits the contemporary interdisciplinary and multidisciplinary pursuits being encouraged in many education systems world over. It can also be used as a textbook and will constitute required reading and texts in many courses offered at school level.

HOW TO USE THE BOOK

Each chapter in the book begins with an African, Chinese, English or Greek proverb aimed at teaching the reader. Every tale/story in this book contains an entrepreneurial characteristic or quality. There is no sequence for reading the stories. In other words, no story is a prerequisite for the other so they can be read in any order. For every story, the entrepreneurial characteristic that it covers is shown in the heading of the section of the story. Some headings have more than one story under them. Chapter 18 concludes the book by using a well-known story of the Bible to illustrate that God has endowed all of us with certain talents and these talents should be creatively and optimally utilized. Chapter 18 concludes the book.

BEFORE USING THE STORY

As an educator, parent, community leader, youth or child caretaker, before you use the story, decide which entrepreneurial characteristic you want to instil in children or you plan to apply in your present life situation. The entrepreneurial characteristics are enlisted in Table 2, chapter 3 in the text.

Ask yourself:

- What do I want the child/pupil/student or myself to learn?
- How will this story help me, the child/pupil/student connect to the real world?
- How do I want the child/pupil/student to think of and apply at the end of the "lesson"?

To be able to answer these questions you will have to read the story in advance before reading it to your audience (or asking your audience to read it if they have to read by themselves). When reading the story make sure that:

- You identify the problem in the story
- Identify the main and other characters in the story
- Think of various solutions to the problem
- Relate to the lesson learned in the story

AFTER READING THE STORY

After reading the story:

Identify characters in the story – the good, the bad and why

- Discuss characters. During the discussion you become a facilitator and encourager, not judge (asking prompting questions like: "What does someone else think about that?" "Why do people think about that?" "What did you mean by...?"). Focus on higher order learning questions beginning with what, how and why.

- Ask specific questions about events or characters from the story. Questions such as "why do you think this happened?", "why did the hare do that?" or "how do you think the tortoise felt?" are good examples. Try to get your audience to "analyze" the story - to think about why something happened and its consequences, the motivations and thinking of characters, etc.

- Relate the story to known life experiences. This is important because by doing so they will assimilate the lesson(s) of the story. It becomes more real and personal for them. Ask questions like "how would you feel if..." or "do you ever feel like [character]?" Why did the hare? Etc.

- Have them get physical. Besides getting them to think, you can get them to act out the story, perhaps even creating their own version of it. This way they will really feel like the story and its lessons are a part of them. Other ways of going physical include letting the students/children retell or summarize the story to demonstrate understanding; letting them produce through drawing, symbols, letters, and writing what in the story caught their interest; letting them tell you/others what lessons they learned from the story; letting them create puppets to demonstrate recognition of the character(s) in the story and use them to retell the story.

- Have them relate the story to their own experiences. After you get them to relate the story to their own experiences, you can really expand their mind by having them relate the story to the larger world. Explain and discuss the entrepreneurial lessons suggested at the end of the story. What else can you add to the lessons and why?

- Put the students or trainees in groups and let them discuss the questions at the end of each chapter. These could also be carry-home assignments for pupils to discuss at home and bring feedback to class.

PART TWO

Inculcating Entrepreneurship Values among Children and the Youths

CHAPTER TWO

WHAT IS YOUTH ENTREPRENEURSHIP?

- *"Eshibishe neshilie" (That which is hidden is precious, go for it). African proverb.*
- *"Eshikhaya shiuma omusala" (A vacuum has no medicine, fill it). African proverb*
- *"Eyisakula ibotsa" (The hen that scratches the ground may find something to eat"). African proverb*

The importance of entrepreneurship to any economy need not be overemphasized. Wealth and a high majority of jobs are created by small businesses started by entrepreneurially minded individuals, many of whom go on to create big businesses. People exposed to entrepreneurship frequently express that they have more opportunity to exercise creative freedoms, higher self-esteem, and an overall greater sense of control over their own lives. As a result, many experienced and successful business people, political leaders, economists, and educators believe that fostering a robust entrepreneurial culture will maximize individual and collective economic and social success on a local, national, and global scale.

When should, and how can, an entrepreneurial culture be fostered among the populace? The phrase, "Youth entrepreneurship" seems to provide a partial answer to this question. The culture should be developed from as early as primary school level (Nafukho, 1997a). The authors can visualize some readers pondering whether it is necessary to introduce children to entrepreneurship yet they are too young to start their own businesses. Bill Gates, founder of Microsoft, began computing at age 13 and by age 17, he had sold his first program – a timetabling system for the school which earned him $4,200 (Kshs.378,000) (http://news.bbc. co.uk/2/hi/business/3428721.stm). In the case of Africa, there are many other examples of individuals who started nurturing business ideas at a very young age. The trouble is that they are not documented so we cannot know them. In the authors' opinion it is the "how" to foster the culture at low levels that becomes an issue. In many African societies, folk tales, proverbs, riddles, and storytelling were a norm among African societies. The tales served several purposes including:

1. Instilling and building of strong characters among the youth. Through tales the youth would learn or be advised about the right behaviour as they grew up. This would be done through stories of people or animals considered heroes/sheroes and therefore role models in the society. The tales would tell of consequences of those who failed to live right by not living according to the values and norms of the society. They would also tell the rewards acquired by those who lived as advised by the older people.

2. A form of passing on knowledge to the younger generations on origins of norms and values of the society.

The authors of this book strongly believe that folklores are still very rich sources for learning important lessons in day-to-day dealings in our lives. From the entrepreneurship point of view they can be used to inculcate an entrepreneurship culture among children, the youth and even among adults. In the case of the contemporary African society, the folk tales and stories are not in a written format. When the grandparents die, they die with their wisdom in the form of stories, folk tales and proverbs. It is with this in mind that the idea of this book was conceived: to prepare children, youth and adults to succeed in entrepreneurship based on African Indigenous Knowledge Systems (AIKS). This book contains tales narrated to the authors when they were young by their grandparents, mothers, fathers and their primary school teachers. (We must hasten to add that we have read and heard of some of them from many other sources including the Bible). The tales in this book depict entrepreneurial characteristics crafted by the authors from the thirteen letters of the word "ENTREPRENEURS" as discussed in Chapter 4 of this book. Before we answer the question posed in the title to this chapter let us ask a few other basic questions, "What is Entrepreneurship? Who is an entrepreneur? What are the benefits of entrepreneurship to the individual and society? How does entrepreneurship develop?"

There are no universally accepted answers to the posed questions. Entrepreneurship may be understood as a process or an event that introduces a new product, a new product method, new markets or a new form of organization, new way of doing things and new way of thinking. These actions help generate wealth. Simply stated, therefore, entrepreneurship is the process of generating viable business ideas, developing them and finally turning them into reality by starting a business venture (Mburugu & Thiong'o, 1991). When understood this way entrepreneurship becomes a process consisting of stages as we shall learn later.

A largely held view of the term "entrepreneur" is that he/she is a person who brings about a change and possesses characteristics to implement ideas to directly benefit him/her and eventually the organization, community and society as a whole. Entrepreneurs traverse all spheres of life including business, education and politics. From the social-economic and business perspectives an entrepreneur is a person who has determination to be self-employed and even employ others. Thus, a true entrepreneur is one who combines factors of production (capital, land, labour and management) such that they will generate greater output. This greater output comes from various input factors and result in wealth creation.

The benefits of entrepreneurship may be divided into three distinct categories that include the benefits to the individual, benefit to society and benefit to the nation. When we teach entrepreneurship we always tell our students that *"nobody gets to be a millionaire working for another."* The message here is that when you work for another person you will always get only part of the profit you create for your employer, who is often an entrepreneur. The employer will remain richer than you. Here, therefore, we see the benefits of entrepreneurship to the individual – to make the individual an own boss and genuinely rich.

When entrepreneurs create business ventures they buy and use inputs, including labour, from within their communities. They therefore create employment and this is of great benefit to society. In the process of generating wealth, entrepreneurs are taxed. A tax is a source of income for the nation and is used to produce public goods such as defence, education, medical care, road infrastructures, and herein lays the importance of entrepreneurship to the nation.

But just how does entrepreneurship develop? Why are some people more entrepreneurial than others? A lot of it lies in the entrepreneurship culture of a people. We believe that an entrepreneurship culture develops in stages. First there is the formative stage. This is followed by the development stage then the start-up stage and finally the growth stage (Ashmore, 1990).

The *Formative Stage* relates to the various factors (including cultural and environmental) that instil an entrepreneurship culture and influence the development of the desire for people and especially the young people to become entrepreneurs as well as attributes and attitudes that are highly related to entrepreneurial success. At this stage, of importance is to encourage young people to acquire appropriate entrepreneurial motivations, attitudes, attributes, behaviours, and values.

The *Developmental Stage* relates to the specific learning and targeted skill development that will equip and prepare an individual to identify and screen a business idea. These are learning skills and strategic skills. Learning skills relate to the willingness and ability of a person to acquire information, knowledge, and experience from the world around them that is relevant to their entrepreneurial success. On the other hand, strategic skills relate to how a person sees the world, envisions what is possible/desirable, and identifies entrepreneurial opportunities in the world around them. This stage is accelerated if an individual went through the formative stage. Unfortunately not many of African youth go through the formative stage.

The *Start-up Stage* refers to the specific skills that are relevant for the successful launch of a business. These are tactical skills for start-up. Tactical skills are important to conceptualising a business, developing a business plan and establishing, launching, and operating a business. A successful start-up stage will very much depend on the development stage which in turn will largely, though not exclusively, depend on the formative stage.

The *Growth Stage* refers to the specific skills that are relevant for a successful entrepreneur who is looking to advance an entrepreneurial venture to a period of growth and expansion. It can be concluded that a key challenge for youth entrepreneurship institutions and programmes is to create an entrepreneurship culture among the youth i.e. to focus on the formative stage.

Meaning of Youth Entrepreneurship

Youth entrepreneurship is the process whereby the youth become aware of business ownership as an option or viable career, develop ideas for business, learn the process of becoming an entrepreneur and undertake the initiation and development of a business. As already stated this is a four stage process involving the formative, development, start-up and growth stages. The factors at play at each stage and a proposal of how to address them are outlined in Table 1. The stories in this book are designed to contribute to the formative stage of Table 1.

Table 1: Stages of Entrepreneurship and the Key Factors at Play

Stage	Key Factors at Play	How to Address the Factors
Formative	COMMUNITY CULTURE The attributes of the environments within which we live, work, and play and the extent to which they encourage, or enable the development of entrepreneurial initiative. The extent to which the "seed" is planted, that is, the desire, want, or engine that lies at the heart of our entrepreneurial potential and motivates a person to want to be an entrepreneur. **The Question Becomes – How Does the Community Culture Impact on Entrepreneurship?**	Public entrepreneurship awareness campaigns through various media such as radio, print media, TV, barazas, and church. Efforts to create an entrepreneurial spirit and culture among the populace, stories and tales about entrepreneurial ventures, role models
Develop-mental	LEARNING AND STRATEGIC SKILLS The willingness and ability of a person to acquire information, knowledge, and experience from the world around him/her that is relevant to his/her entrepreneurial success. His/her vision: how a person sees the world, envisions what is possible/desirable, and identifies entrepreneurial opportunities in the world around him/her	Basic entrepreneurship skills teaching in schools. Inculcating the entrepreneurship culture in the youth while at school – making the youth view self-employment as an alternative employment avenue.

Start-up	TACTICAL SKILLS 1 The skills that are important to conceptualizing a business, developing a business plan and establishing, launching, and operating a business	Business start-up skills for post school graduates including drop-outs. Self-employment promotion policies; creation of youth business incubation programmes; financing; mentoring; and organizing youth entrepreneur's competitions.
Growth	TACTICAL SKILLS 2 The skills that are important to moving a successful business into and through a period of growth and expansion	Business growth and expansion skills for practicing entrepreneurs; financing; mentoring; and organizing youth entrepreneur's competitions

---

REFLECTION QUESTIONS

1. How can entrepreneurship contribute to the popular advice given to the youth *that, "you are leaders of tomorrow"?*
2. What are some of the shortcomings of youth development programmes in Africa and how can they be overcome?
3. What do you think are the main contributions of indigenous knowledge systems to the learning of entrepreneurship? Why?
4. *What* contributions do entrepreneurs in your community make to people, region, and country?

CHAPTER THREE

HOW CAN OUR CHILDREN BECOME SUCCESSFUL ENTREPRENEURS?

- *"Eyilikhumala likhuchakanga butoro"* (A champion bull starts from birth). African proverb.
- *What I hear I forget; what I see I remember; what I do I understand.* (Chinese Proverb).

THE SQUIRREL AND THE SPIDER

A long time ago on this earth lived two friends: Mr. Squirrel and Mr. Spider. Mr. Spider's daughter got married up above the world in "heaven". Time came when the spider was to visit his in laws in "heaven". Being a faithful friend of the squirrel the spider invited the squirrel to accompany him. "My friend", said the squirrel when he was invited, "You know I do not have legs and a web like yours to be able to go anywhere like you. I am afraid I cannot accompany you." The spider replied, "A friend in need is a friend indeed. You are my good friend. Do not worry about your inabilities. Just climb on my back and I will carry you." The squirrel obliged.

As the spider made its web and climbed towards "heaven" the creative mind of the squirrel went overdrive imagining all the goodies the hosts must have prepared for the visitors from far away. "My friend," called out the squirrel from the spider's back. "You see "heaven" is not earth. They do everything differently there and even their names are not the earthly names. We should change our names to fit in their environment" because when you go to Rome you must act as Romans do. The spider agreed but invited the squirrel to employ his wit to manufacture the fitting names to which the squirrel gladly agreed and announced that his name will be – "The visitors" while the spider will be – "The visitor".

As they approached the edge of heaven and earth they heard the hosts' children shouting out – the visitors are here, the visitors are here. The squirrel whispered to the spider, "They have seen me on your back. They are calling out my name." The faithful spider believed Mr. Squirrel.

When they arrived in "heaven" they were escorted to a well laid out room while food was being prepared in an adjacent room. Eventually they heard the hosts telling the servers to go and serve food to the visitors. As you must have guessed the squirrel convinced the spider that it was to be his food and that the spider should wait for his serving. The squirrel enjoyed all the food and anything that was being offered in the name of visitors. The hosts interpreted the silence and inactivity by Mr. Spider to mean that he was only obeying his earthly culture as the real in-law.

Eventually time to leave came and the announcement was, "let us escort the visitors back home". At that time the spider told the squirrel, "of course it is you being escorted. So go well my friend. As for me it will now be my turn to get attention." The squirrel had no option but to go alone. At the edge of "heaven" and earth the squirrel had no option but to jump down there being nobody to carry him to descend down to earth. The fall was so heavy that the squirrel fainted and went into a coma.

Along came a woman carrying a child in a bag of nuts on her back and saw the dead aka fainted squirrel. She thanked the heavens for availing the juicy meat and took the squirrel and put it in the bag on her back and continued on her home bound journey. Within no time the squirrel recovered from his faint and started eating the nuts in the bag. The child informed the mother about this but the mother ignored the child's alert in an adult-dismiss-child manner of "the children are there to be seen and not to be heard" common in many societies. When the squirrel had had his fill he jumped out of the bag and disappeared in the bush. Arriving at home the woman noticed there were neither nuts nor the squirrel in the bag.

LESSONS

A number of lessons can be learned from this story. At the end of it we learn that adults can ignore the youth at their own peril. This is particularly true of youth entrepreneurship. We ignore it at the expense of inclusive national development. The story also tells us that in partnership the unfaithful partner takes unwarranted risks as the squirrel did. It also warns us that over-creativity can be counterproductive as was the case with the squirrel.

And now here are some interesting answers from three children aged between 4-9 concerning entrepreneurship whom the authors interacted with in Kenya.

Question; suppose I give you money, how best would you utilize it?

Answer 1; buy mummy a house like our neighbour's

Answer 2; buy daddy a big lorry to accommodate more sacks of maize.

Answer 3; buy a "matatu" to carry passengers.

Each of the three children built the answer on their background, upbringing and surrounding environment. The first one reflected on his environment and wished to invest in real estate because that was the norm in the neighbourhood yet his single mother did not have one. The second opted for a lorry since she reckoned the pick up used by the dad in transporting grains to the market was small. The third one believed he must be a driver, like his uncle, who makes a comfortable living out of being a *'matau'* driver.

The implication is that the environment they live in (what they hear and see) dictates much of what they wish to do and their aspiration to make better the situation. This tells us that the three children are business oriented since people around them in one way or the other practise the same. They want to imitate what the parents do.

On the other hand, their dreams can be realized if the parents take the initiative to nurture such aspirations. The big question remains, how many parents have time off their schedules to share in their children dreams, how many realize the need to mould the child on what is good at a young age? In reality, we know that school teachers spend most of their time with our children. This means that they have a critical role to play in instilling entrepreneurial culture. Thus, parents and teachers have a role to play in arousing and nurturing the interests of the young to grow up responsibly and entrepreneurially. Parents and teachers are the most instrumental group in adding quality to the ideas of the young ones; their encouragement and support is recipe for the end product-the young entrepreneur.

But why bother the parent and the primary and secondary school teacher with instilling entrepreneurship culture? Kenya, like many other developing nations in Africa, has more primary schools than secondary schools and more secondary schools than tertiary institutions. At every successive level there are graduates and drop-outs who seek for wage employment in vain. They seek for wage employment because their upbringing has inculcated a wage-employment culture in them. Parents and the teachers have urged them to study hard to join secondary school and on to university to get a good job. The alternative of self-employment and the skills and attitudes to assist them start their own businesses have never been instilled in them.

Can our children become successful entrepreneurs? Research has shown that entrepreneurial traits emerge in children at a very young age; often by the time they hit primary school. We have personally observed nursery school children whether on TV or physically at their schools and can say that some of them posses entrepreneurial qualities such as a taste for risk-taking, creative problem-solving abilities, and high internal motivation to succeed. Unfortunately as these children grow older, many lose that entrepreneurial spark. Only a few of university graduates we have taught posses the said qualities by the time they graduate from the university. The story is not different when it comes to high school graduates.

In order for children to preserve entrepreneurial tendencies into their teenage and adult years, parents and teachers must encourage, support, and facilitate the children's ambitions and endeavours. The tales in this book have the objective of contributing to the entrepreneurship formative stage described earlier. They can be used to identify entrepreneurial characteristics and qualities. In recognition of the fact that there are as many entrepreneurial characteristics and qualities as there are entrepreneurs we use one of the entrepreneurial characteristics – CREATIVITY – to craft thirteen characteristics of entrepreneurs from the very word – ENTREPRENEURS as shown in Table 2 of Chapter 4.

REFLECTION QUESTIONS

1. At what age should children be taught about money and getting rich and how should it be done?

2. What mistake (if any) did the squirrel make in the story above?

3. Why do you think parents and teachers in Africa should encourage children to be interested in creating their own jobs when they grow up instead of being employed by the Government?

4. What mistake (if any did) the spider make in the above story?

CHAPTER FOUR

LESSONS FOR EVERY "SHOESTRING" ENTREPRENEUR

- *"Eyibula amakhwana yisika amabere" (The cow that calves twins must also produce enough milk to feed them or a successful entrepreneur must be prepared to manage success). African proverb.*

- *"Eyirulile shiiritsanga" (There should be no fear once you have set off on an errand or mission). African proverb.*

A common answer entrepreneurship scholars have gotten from people for having not started their own businesses is lack of capital. Indeed starting a business requires adequate capital. However, our personal observations and researches do reveal that capital alone is not a guarantee for entrepreneurial success. While some businesses start out with millions in the coffers and end up nowhere, there are others who start with shoestring budgets but eventually grow to become very successful.

Dunn (1978, p.1) quotes E. F. Schumacher, author of "Small is Beautiful" as having taught that:

"If you want to go places, start from where you are.
If you are poor start with something cheap.
If you are uneducated start with something relatively simple.
If you live in a poor environment and poverty makes markets small start with something small.
If you are unemployed, start using your labour power because any productive use of it is better than letting it lie idle.
In other words we must learn to recognize boundaries of poverty. A project that does not fit, educationally or organizationally, into the environment, will be an economic failure and a cause of disruption".

Success in entrepreneurship does not necessarily depend on how fat the wallet is at the beginning of the business. Rather, it is an exercise of smart financial management, careful strategic planning and many other characteristics that we discuss in this book. In the next section of this chapter, we propose thirteen ways an entrepreneur on a tight budget can still come out a winner.

1. Set realistic goals.

One of the first steps every start-up entrepreneur must do is to determine the right scope and size of his/her business. Many entrepreneurs fail to envisage i.e. plan ahead and simply jump into the idea of starting a business, without understanding what the business really entails and they eventually fall short of what they can really do. We call this group of entrepreneurs "me-too syndromers" who simply ape others already in business without analyzing the main variables involved.

2. Plan your costs properly.

A lot of people start a business without the faintest idea of what the costs will be. They either overestimate the cost, or worse, underestimate the financial requirements needed to properly capitalize the business. We know of many small scale business owners who never think of the cost of licences and end up in conflict with the law.

3. Smart financing for your business.

Sources of finance for a business can be varied. For many entrepreneurs, there is no single source to finance their entire operation. The money provided by one source (e.g. from family and friends) may be enough to buy your raw materials, but you still need money for your working capital. Entrepreneurs need to network well to source finances.

4. Put your money where it will bear fruit.

Shoestring entrepreneurs have one common characteristic: they lack money and often struggle to raise capital for their businesses. Capital of a start-up venture goes to either of these investments: "fixed assets" (furniture, fixtures, and equipment), or "working assets" (inventory and working capital). Despite the lack of capital, many small business owners we have met put most of their money to buying fancy equipment and "cool" office space - costs that a struggling start-up can do without. This is a common error in business decision-making. Successful business owners put as much money as possible into the working assets - which bears cash and sales - and as little as possible into fixed assets.

5. Is it the right time?

Timing can be a key to the success of a start-up. There's a right time and a wrong time to open a business, especially if your business is cyclical in nature or in a seasonal location. It is very much like buying shares. Timing the buying and selling is crucial to financial success.

6. Control the cash.

Cash flow is said to be the lifeblood of a small business. Your business will survive only as long as it has the cash to pay for your financial obligations. With limited capital, cash flow controls every decision in shoestring enterprise, and it can be the only way to navigate during your start-up phase. One mistake many business people make is to mistake cash for profit and start using it even before the business breaks even. To breakeven one has to endure.

7. Push the sales.

Building sales depend on several factors - nature of the business, location, level or competition, and intensity of marketing and promotion. The goal of every shoestring entrepreneur must be to build up sales immediately. If you have financed your business on borrowed money you must pay it back as promised. You therefore need to push the marketing of your business. The key rule is to dedicate at least two hours of your day to marketing your business. Know the steps you will take before you open and after you open to maximize sales and help the business to first increase its sales.

8. Balance your sales and profit objectives.

Sales and profit do not always go together. Some entrepreneurs are willing to cut down their profits in their effort to drive sales up. Oftentimes volume alone will not be able to compensate for the loss in profits. Strive to give the business the best balance between a solid policy of capturing sales without sacrificing needed profit margins. To do this you must have a strong need to achieve.

9. Be 'lean and mean'.

A struggling start-up does not need dead weights. Be efficient. Keep your fixed costs down, and spend only on items that can sufficiently contribute to improving the bottom line. If for example you can still adequately operate from your home (say baking and delivering to supermarkets), there is little need in leasing an office space in the town area. Avoid hiring a permanent employee if you can still make do with temporary and seasonal staffs. Every shilling in expense should be directly tied to income: spend a cent only when you are sure you can get a shilling in return.

10. Master the financial tools.

As a business owner, you are responsible for the life and growth of your business. This entails knowing, not only the marketing or production aspects of your business, but the financial tools you need to manage your business effectively. Understanding the finances of your business will give you control over its direction. This may be difficult to some entrepreneurs, but knowing your business records will tell you where you have been, where you are going, and how fast you are getting there. Sure, you can hire bookkeepers and accountants. But you yourself need to understand your cash flow, income, profit and loss statements, and break-even point.

11. Be prepared to work smart and hard.

Profit must be earned. Very often the day of an entrepreneur starts earlier and ends later than that of a wage-employed or ordinary person. This requires both psychological and physical strength and energy.

12. Keep innovating.

If you keep doing what you always do you will keep getting what you always got. You can not beat competitors if you are not doing things better or more differently than them. Even when there are no competitors, customer preferences change with time and you must read this and keep with it. Creativity and innovation is the blood in the veins of successful entrepreneurs.

13. Believe in what you do.

Business is about risk and risk taking is one of the key characteristics of entrepreneurs. Entrepreneurs do not gamble. They take calculated risks, believe in themselves and never look back.

We can now summarize these lessons into thirteen entrepreneurial characteristics coined from the word "ENTREPRENEURS" as shown in Table 2.

Table 2. Bwisa's Entrepreneurial Characteristics

	Character	Meaning
\multicolumn{3}{l}{ENTREPRENEURS ARE:}		
E	Envisaging	Have dreams of foresight. Plan ahead; set **S**pecific **M**easurable **A**chievable **R**ealistic **T**ime bound goals.
N	Networking	Are good organizers of factors of production; bringing together people and other components of a venture. Create productive relations with suppliers, customers and other stakeholders, including their competitors.
T	Time-conscious	Look at time as money. Hate wasting time on things that are unimportant. Take timely decisions.
R	Realistic	Do not build castles in the air; do not bite more than you can chew.
E	Energetic	Are full of energy of both the mind and the body. Take good care of their bodies and refuse to overindulge
P	Planners	Avoid the me-too syndrome i.e. merely aping other businesspeople. Carefully think about what you want to do, why you want to do and when you want to do it.
R	Result-oriented	Profit is their goal. Focus on customer care that gives results
E	Efficiency-oriented	Hate wasting resources; use resources optimally to achieve maximum results.
N	N-arch	Have a strong desire to achieve.
E	Enduring	Tolerate long hours of work; tolerate ambiguity; work hard to overcome obstacles.
U	Unstoppable	Optimism: Live by the philosophy that this is the best of times, and that anything is possible. Describe a glass as half full not half way or half empty
R	Responsible	Acceptance of responsibility: Are morally, legally, and mentally accountable for their ventures. Uphold business ethics.
S	Self-confident	Confidently and carefully plan their work and work their plans.

REFLECTION QUESTIONS

1. How possibly can one start a business with no cash and which type of business could it be?

2. Modern researchers in entrepreneurship think that money is not the biggest road block to business start up. Do you agree with them? Why?

3. What mistakes should a beginning entrepreneur avoid to ensure success?

4. What behavioral traits should those planning to go into business learn?

PART THREE

Entrepreneurial Characteristics: Proverbs, Stories and Lessons Learned

CHAPTER FIVE

ENTREPRENEURS ENVISAGING

- "Chenda kaala yola ehale" (A slow but sure traveller reaches far). African proverb.

- *Munyal deefan hayre.* Patience can cook a stone (African Proverb)

- *He who fails to plan; plans to fail (English proverb).*

THE RABBIT AND THE CHAMELEON

Once upon a time a rabbit and a chameleon were invited for a party. Both were very happy and the rabbit started to ridicule and laugh at the chameleon because the party was in a distant land. The shrewd rabbit planned to trick the chameleon. He told the chameleon that the first person to arrive will be the one to enjoy the party alone. The Chameleon knew he would not beat the rabbit at speed so he thought he would not try anyway. However, the thought of the good food at the party and all the enjoyment that goes with it was overwhelming. The more he imagined about the loss of all these goodies the more his mind went into overdrive thinking of a plan. Somewhere at the back of his mind something was telling the chameleon that he needed a good plan.

Finally an idea struck him - to use advantage of his light weight and ride on the hairy tail of the rabbit. He therefore challenged the rabbit who really scoffed at him. Come the visiting day and the chameleon challenged the rabbit to start ahead of him. This meant that the rabbit was to stand in front of the chameleon to start. The light chameleon then silently jumped onto the tail of the rabbit as the rabbit was taking off.

The rabbit ran very fast as the chameleon sat comfortably on the rabbit's tail and enjoyed the ride. When the rabbit arrived and was given a chair to sit down the chameleon shouted, "DO NOT SIT ON ME I AM ALREADY SEATED HERE!" The rabbit was so scared and ashamed that he couldn't celebrate in the party.

LESSON

To envisage is to look ahead; to make plans for achieving goals. All business people plan but some plan well than others. For example, the chameleon in the above story did. Both the rabbit and the chameleon planned but the chameleon had a better plan. The story also tells us that entrepreneurs should be strategic in facing the competition. The Chameleon was very tactical and strategic in the way he handled the rabbit. The story further tells us that entrepreneurs must always identify their competitive advantage. The Chameleon knew he didn't have an advantage over the rabbit in terms of speed but realized that his light weight was an advantage. With patience and restraint, one can solve even the most difficult problems.

Solar Power Dreams that Became a Reality

As learned in this chapter, entrepreneurs are *Envisaging*. When confronted with an issue they think and dream of possible solutions. Then they set realistic plans of how to address the problem. As a child growing up in Western Kenya, Evans Wadongo struggled to do his homework by using a kerosene lamp which was deem and did not provide bright light necessary for reading. He was caned at school if his family ran out of fuel for the lamp and he could not do his homework. He permanently damaged his eyesight by sitting over the smoky fumes that came from the kerosene lamp.

His father was a strict teacher and his greatest inspiration and ensured that Evans completed school to join Jomo Kenyatta University of Agriculture and Technology (JKUAT) to pursue Electronic and Computer Engineering degree.

At the university Evans' misery of using a smoky kerosene lamp to study were buried and forgotten. He had plenty of light to use. What he did not forget, though, were the many children in the villages who were struggling with kerosene lamps like he did. He envisaged, dreamed and started wondering how to improve reading conditions for children in rural communities similar to his home village - and there are many in Kenya and indeed in Africa.

At an early age of 19 in 2004 and while at JKUAT Evans designed and invented a solar lamp which he calls *Mwanga Bora* (Swahili for good light) after using part of his student loan to buy what he needed. His initial idea was to make just one lamp and take to his own family. In 2004, as a way to address poor education, climate change, health and poverty in rural areas in Kenya. Evans named the entire project 'Use Solar, Save Lives' Program, as he aimed to use solar technology as a way to save lives in poor communities. However by 2004 Evans had produced some 15,000 solar laps. His goal is to produce 100,000 by 2015. For Evans the lamps are not an end in themselves, but rather "a way to lift people out of poverty." It is a dream come true.

Evans has constituted a team for a project called "Use Solar, Save Lives". The team identifies impoverished communities that rely for lighting on kerosene lamps. They hand out lamps to the community members who are often a women's group, and encourage them to pool the money they would have used to buy the kerosene to start entrepreneurial activities.

In recognition of Evans Wandongo's invention of solar lamps, he was selected as a Cable News Network (CNN) Top Ten Hero for 2010, among over 10,000 nominations worldwide. He was honoured at an All Star Tribute show in Hollywood by Oscar winning actress, Halle Berry. The show was graced by top celebrities in entertainment and business and included performances by Sugarland, Bon Jovi and John Legend. The show was broadcast all over the world by the Cable News Network (CNN).

Evans is also a winner for the inaugural 'Man who changed the world award' in honour of former Soviet Union president and Nobel winner, Mikhail Gorbachev. Other winners are CNN founder Ted Turner, and World Wide Web (WWW) inventors Tim Bemers-Lee and Robert Cailliau.

Evans Wadongo and his story has been featured on CNN, BBC, AFP, France 24, MBC South Korea, K24 TV, NTV, Citizen TV, KBC TV, German Radio, KISS FM, Capital FM, Radio Jambo, Nation Newspaper, The Star newspaper, The People newspaper, Passion magazine, Parents magazine, Management magazine and several online news sources. His story is therefore in the public domain.

At below 25 years of age Evans has already changed the lives of tens of thousands of people living in poor rural communities in Africa by supplying them with solar lamps produced from pieces of fabricated scrap metal and discarded solar equipment. Evans has joined the ranks of great social entrepreneurs in the world.

REFLECTION QUESTIONS

1. What mistake did the rabbit make to be defeated by the slow chameleon?

2. What risks did the chameleon take in planning to do what he did?

3. How you would design a creative plan to address the challenge the chameleon in the story above faced?

4. Why should one always think of alternative ways of addressing challenges?

5. Like Evans Wandongo, think of an issue you have faced in your life that needs to be solved and discuss how this problem can be addressed and what would be your role in addressing the problem?

CHAPTER SIX

ENTREPRENEURS NETWORKING

- *"Niwenya okhutsia lwangu chenda wenyene, niwenya okhula ehale, chenda nabashio" (If you want to go fast and achieve less, then walk alone; but if you want to go far and achieve more in life, walk or work with others) African Proverb.*

- *It takes a village to raise a child (African proverb).*

- *If you want happiness for an hour -- take a nap. If you want happiness for a day -- go fishing. If you want happiness for a month -- get married. If you want happiness for a year -- inherit a fortune. If you want happiness for a lifetime -- help someone else. (Chinese Proverb).*

TORTOISES HUNTING OSTRICHES

It is said that once in the wilderness the Tortoises held a meeting to discuss how they might hunt Ostriches. They resolved that they would all stand next to each other on both sides of the path where the ostriches passed and let one of them go to ambush the ostriches. When the Ostriches were ambushed they had to flee along the path through the midst of tortoises." The tortoises were many. As the ostriches ran for their dear lives the tortoises who could not run at all did not move but remained always in the same places but kept calling each other, "Are you there?" and each one answered, "I am here." The Ostriches hearing this, ran faster and faster until they exhausted their strength, and fell down. Then the Tortoises assembled by-and-by at the place where the Ostriches had fallen, and had a good meal for days and weeks.

KING DOVE AND THE DOVES

Once upon a time, there lived many doves in the jungle. One day they went out in search of food. They flew long distances but did not get anything to eat. All of them were now completely exhausted.

A young dove asked the King Dove, "Your majesty, please permit us to take some rest."

The King replied, "Have courage, my dear young fellow. We shall definitely get something to eat very soon."

The young dove started flapping his wings with force and soon left everyone behind.

After sometime, he turned back and spoke to others, "Hey, I see lots of grains down there."

Hearing this, all the doves started rushing towards the scattered rice under a tree. Suddenly the King Dove said, "It is too good to be true. There is something amiss. Don't rush towards the grains, it may be a trick. Some hunter must have laid a trap."

But the doves did not listen at all. The sight of the grains was too tempting. Without giving a thought to the King's advice, they swooped down and started eating the grains. After having their fill they tried to fly only to realise that they were caught in a net.

The King Dove said, "I told you before that it is a trick of some hunter."

All of them felt ashamed and scared.

One of them said, "O, King of doves, kindly save us. We're sorry for what we did. This has happened for the first time with us. We won't do it again. Do anything but just save us."

So the King Dove said , "all of you must try to fly with the net in unison, all of you."

Just then they saw a hunter approaching towards them. The King Dove said, "Now all of you, fly together".

So all the doves flapped their wings together and flew with the net. The hunter stood dazed. He couldn't believe what he had just seen. As the doves approached a temple, the King Dove said, "Get down near the temple. A rat, who is an old friend of mine, lives there. He will nibble the net with his sharp teeth and get us free."

So everyone was thrilled at their success. They headed for the temple and descended near it along with the net. Then the King Dove called the rat, "Oh! my friend! Come out and help us. We are in trouble."

The rat recognised his friend's voice. He peeped out of his hole. He said, "Just wait for some time, I'll call some of my friends who will set you free." Saying so he went to get his friends.

After sometime a number of rats came and began to nibble the net. They nibbled all the strings of the net. Soon the rats set the doves free. The doves thanked the rats and flew back to their nests.

LESSONS LEARNT

Unity developed through social networking and team work is strength. The network of tortoises helped them defeat the fast running ostriches and it is only when the doves acted in unison that they were able to fly away with the net they had been trapped in. In business, social networks and business alliances are useful. Avoid destructive competition and/or isolation.

Iko Toilet - Solving a Social Problem Using Networking & Social Entrepreneurial Strategies

David Kuria an architect by profession added value to the concept of using a toilet in the city of Nairobi through the entrepreneurship principle of networking and using business strategies and techniques to solve a social problem in an entrepreneurial way. He came up with an idea aimed at ensuring that trips to city toilets were both pleasant and memorable for the toilet users. How did he achieve his mission? Well, he dreamed of transforming the idea that city toilets were not all about filth and rot envisioned in most people's minds based on their experiences using public toilets in the city. Disturbed by lack of toilets in most towns and informal settlements in Kenya and concerned for the welfare of low income people in the city, he quit a well-paying job as an architect with a non-governmental organization to engage in 'toilet' business. He wanted to serve the poor who are the majority in the city of Nairobi. Those who could not afford to eat in luxury city hotels and therefore access toilets with running water. As a start, Mr. Kuria made solid waste management his entry point. While working for the NGO, he learned social networking skills and utilized the skills by raising funds for people who had taken up garbage recycling. By doing this, he became part of the solution to the sanitation problems of the majority. He aimed at developing ecologically friendly toilets which he named 'Iko', which is a convenient version of ecological. The word Iko in Swahili means *there is,* therefore *Iko* toilet, means there is a toilet for your use.

Kuria's entrepreneurial mind led to the development of the award-winning Iko-toilet, a concept that envisions the idea of a "toilet mall" where toilets are availed at the modest cost of Sh5 ($.05), as well as shops that stock snacks and barber shops. Piped music is also offered. Kuria's entrepreneurial idea and implementation framework, social, economic and political influencing strategy has won the following awards:

- Guinness World Record 2010
- UN Dubai International Best Practices Award 2010
- Africa Social Enterprise of the Year 2009 by World Economic Forum
- Ashoka Fellowship on Public Innovation for 2008;
- Lemelson Fellowship on technological innovations;
- World Toilet Organization Hall of Fame 2008;
- Schwab Fellowship on social entrepreneurship 2009;
- Citation by President Bill Clinton during the Clinton Global Initiative 2009.

REFLECTION QUESTIONS

1. Like David Kuria in the Iko Toliet story above, think of a social issue in your community that needs to be solved and discuss how this problem can be addressed and what would be your role in addressing the problem?

2. How can families in a village use their numbers to their advantage?

3. What types of group activities can pupils in a class engage in to benefit them?

4. Why do you think entrepreneurs like doves in the story "the King and Doves" need to have a network of trusted friends?

5. How can school management motivate students to stay in school and not drop out? How can you encourage your friends to continue with schooling?

CHAPTER SEVEN

EN**T**REPRENEURS **T**IME CONSCIOUSNESS

- *You love what you find time to do (Anonymous).*

- *People who never have time on their hands are those who do the least. (Source:* <u>Georg C. Lichtenberg</u> *(1742-1799) German scientist, satirist and anglophile).*

- *Time is the most valuable coin in your life. You and you alone will determine how that coin will be spent. Be careful that you don't let other people spend it for you. (Source:* <u>John Dryden</u> *(1631-1700) British poet, dramatist and critic).*

THE TORTOISE AND THE HARE

A tortoise and a hare once got into an argument about who could run faster. They decided that the best way to settle the matter was to have a race, so they agreed on a time and a place to meet and then went their separate ways. Hare was so confident that he was going to win that he didn't bother to start at the agreed time. Instead he decided to take a nap. He told himself that when he woke, he could easily overtake the tortoise and win the race. The tortoise, however, started on time. He plodded along, going slowly, but not stopping even once to rest. On and on he went. Eventually, just as the hare was waking up, the tortoise crossed the finish line. The tortoise was slow but he had won the race.

LESSONS LEARNT

Time and tide waits for no man and time is money. Timely actions will get you rewards and success.

THE ANT AND THE GRASSHOPPER

Once upon a time, there lived an Ant and a Grasshopper. One time during the harvest season the Ant started collecting grain that had remained in the fields to his nest. The Grasshopper just ate the grain and hopped about in the field. When the Grasshopper saw the Ant busy carrying away grain he said to him, "Why not come and chat with me instead of toiling and moiling in that way?"

"No," said the Ant. "I am helping to lay up food for the lean season. That is when I will have time to chat and I recommend you to do the same." "Why bother about lean seasons?" said the Grasshopper; "we have got plenty of food at present." But the Ant went on its way and continued its toil. When the lean times came the Grasshopper had no food and found itself dying of hunger, while it saw the Ants distributing every day corn and grain from the stores they had collected during harvest time.

LESSON

There is time for everything. There is time to play and there is time to rest. Entrepreneurs plan their time well and know when to do what; they know that it is best to prepare for the days of necessity.

Making Money from Roasting Maize

Early in the 1990s I (Prof. Bwisa) successfully chaired a committee that introduced entrepreneurship education at Kenya's Jomo Kenyatta University of Agriculture and Technology (JKUAT). In 1994 I realized we were teaching entrepreneurship using cases and examples that are foreign and therefore irrelevant. This made me start a micro business of retailing cooking gas otherwise called LPG (Liquid Petroleum Gas) on the outskirts of Kenya's capital city – Nairobi for the main purpose of using it as my own teaching reference and also supplement my salary. I employed a sixth form graduate who was looking for an opportunity to work and raise fees for a training course. His monthly salary was Ksh. 5000. Soon his brother who had finished form four joined him from upcountry and requested me to secure for him a job - any job. Using my entrepreneurship teaching slogan and philosophy of, "Nobody gets to be a millionaire working for another", I proposed to him that with his level of education he should start roasting maize and grow in the business. I had interviewed a young man who was roasting maize in front of my retail shop who had told me that he earned Ksh. 24,000 ($267) per month roasting the maize. At that time this was equivalent to a salary of a college lecturer and more than that of a police officer. He risked the idea.

His initial investment was Ksh. 200 which I lent him. He used Ksh. 10 to buy a measure of charcoal and assembled the roasting gear from waste. He used Ksh. 20 to travel to and from the commodity market where he used Ksh. 170 to buy 51 raw cobs of maize having been sold 3 cobs for Ksh. 10. He roasted and sold each cob at Ksh. 15 making Ksh. 765 in gross profit in about 3 hours. He gave me back my Ksh. 200

plus 10% interest of Ksh. 20 and remained with Ksh. 545 at the end of that day. The next day the young man used Ksh. 235 to buy 70 cobs and sold them off making a gross profit of Ksh. 1050. By mid-month the young man was selling 90 cobs per day this works out at Ksh. Ksh. 40 500 per month in gross profits. This attracted the elder brother who resigned from my low paying employment and together they joined forces in the business of roasting and selling maize. After some time they had saved enough money to enable them return to their rural homes where they have integrated backwards producing the maize they roast rather than buying from suppliers. This has improved profitability. They have also diversified into horticulture and do plant sugarcane on leased farms. It would appear that for the duo the sky is not even the limit. The two brothers made timely decisions and are now witnessing the benefits of entrepreneurship.

REFLECTION QUESTIONS

1. What does the phrase "time is money" mean to you?

2. What other lessons does the story of the ant and the grasshopper teach us?

3. Explain why an entrepreneur like the ant in the story above should be concerned with saving for the future?

4. Explain how timing was important to the two brothers who are engaged in Maize roasting business.

CHAPTER EIGHT

ENT**R**EPRENEURS **R**EALISTIC

- *"Amakhanga shikapulushira khulala" (Guinea-fowls never fly off at the same time lest their wings collide). African proverb.*

- *"Anangali shayingwa" (Do not compete with your superior). African proverb.*

THE HUNTERS AND THE SMALL BIRD

It is said that once upon a time a hunter caught the swift (a small bird) and took her home. When the hunter was about to kill her for food the bird said to him, "What will it advantage you to kill me? I am so small that I cannot satisfy your appetite. Let me go, and I will give you three rules from which you will derive great benefit, if you follow them accurately." Astonished at hearing the bird speak, he promised her freedom on the conditions she had stated.

"Hear, then," said the bird. "First, never attempt impossibilities. Secondly, do not lament an irrecoverable loss. Thirdly, do not credit things that are incredible. If you keep these three maxims with wisdom, they will infinitely profit you."

The man, faithful to his promise, let the bird escape. As she flew away she said to the hunter, "You are a silly fellow, and have today lost a great treasure. There is in my bowels a pearl bigger than the egg of an ostrich."

Full of annoyance at her escape, he immediately spread his nets and tried to take her a second time, but she eluded the hunter's trap.

"Come into my house, sweet bird," he said, "and I will show you every kindness.

I will feed you with my own hands, and permit you to fly away and come back at your own pleasure and leisure."

The bird answered, "Now I am certain you are a fool, and pay no regard to the wisdom I gave you: 'Regret not what is irrecoverable.' You cannot take me again, yet you have spread your net for that purpose. Moreover, you believe that my bowels contain a pearl larger than the egg of an ostrich, when I myself am nothing near that size! You are a fool, and a fool you will always remain."

With these words she flew away. The man returned sorrowfully to his own house, but never again obtained the sight of the bird.

LESSONS LEARNT

Being realistic is a good business virtue. The ability to scan our own environment with the objective of improving our own situation and those of others is a key entrepreneurial characteristic.

Promise of Wealth

The 19th August 2009 BBC news bulletin caught every listener by surprise. It ran, "Twenty-one-year-old Kenyan Jane Mweni has won the BBC Swahili Faidika na BBC (Prosper with the BBC) young entrepreneur competition and would be invited to address the Youth Forum during November's biennial Commonwealth Heads of Government Meeting (CHOGM) in Trinidad and Tobago."

At the grand final in Mombasa, Kenya, on 13 August 2009, Jane was presented with the US$5,000 prize to help launch her business proposal on waste management in Mombasa.

The business idea that won Mweni the prestigious award was on waste. According to Mweni there is a slum next to where she lives, which is filled with rubbish, because no-one can afford to pay the high fee charged by trash collection companies. So for her project she proposed a company which can still turn over a profit but collect the rubbish at a much lower price. She estimated that with her business all 1,500 households in the slum will pay less than a dollar for the whole month, compared with 8-10 dollars they were being charged by other companies. Her business would employ around 50 young unemployed people.

Mweni's story excited the authors of this book who conducted some basic research and established that about a billion people in our world rely upon wood and charcoal for cooking, resulting in wide-spread deforestation and loss of the world's forests each year. In countries like Kenya where the average income is $1-2 per day, cooking fuel can consume half of a family's income. Fuel briquettes to replace wood and charcoal can be made from readily available waste materials. In urban areas, this can be sawdust and shredded paper. In villages and rural areas, they can be made from leaves, grass, coffee and rice husks and other agricultural waste in many combinations. One can therefore really make money from waste by scanning the environment in a realistic way.

REFLECTION QUESTIONS

1. What real-life situations do you recall that fit the lesson in this story?

2. Why do you think the bird earned her freedom so easily?

3. Why do you think entrepreneurs need freedom to decide how to invest their resources?

4. Why do you think consumers need freedom to decide what goods and services to purchase?

CHAPTER NINE

ENTR**E**PRENEURS
ENERGETIC

- *"Abasusumi bafunana okhukhuura omwikho"* (Idlers struggle to clear food remains from a cooking stick). African proverb. Wambunya, T. (2005, p. 7).
- *Litakho shiluchuma ta* (Buttocks do not bring profit). Meaning, do not spend all your time on the sofa seated instead of working.

MR LAZY

A long time ago in the days of mythology there lived a man known only as Mr. Lazy. He only depended on what astrologers told him. One time he went to see a renowned astrologer for advice. The astrologer examined Mr. Lazy and told him that he would become a millionaire at 40 years old and will live to become a centurion enjoying his riches. Mr. Lazy was so pleased that he danced all the way home from the astrologer's house. From then on, all he did was dream of when he will become a millionaire and did not bother finding work. Finally, he became so poor that he died of hunger at age 39.

After his death, Mr. Lazy went to see the lord of death to file a complaint against the astrologer. The lord of death examined him and was astonished that Mr. Lazy could have died at a young age of 39. Further examination revealed that indeed Mr. Lazy was supposed to have become very rich at 40 years. This made the lord to send his investigators back to earth to investigate the case.

The report was a long one. First it was discovered that the astrologer was accurate. The heavenly emperor had decided to give Mr. Lazy riches through the god of wisdom. When the god of wisdom went down to earth and looked for Mr. Lazy in all the graduation lists of all the schools, colleges and universities, in the hope that he can arrange to pay him the money in the form of a big salary as a very senior civil servant he never found the name of Mr. lazy in any of the graduation lists, nor as a candidate for the civil service examinations. The god of wisdom thought that perhaps Mr. lazy could be in the military services records so he handed over the riches to the god of war to help him out.

The god of war took the money and started looking for Mr. Lazy in all the Military Services, including the Army and the Police. He could not locate Mr. Lazy anywhere in the rank and file either. Unable to help Mr. Lazy to get a big military victory and a big award, he asked the god of wealth for assistance.

The god of wealth, responsible for commercial prosperity, went down to the business world to look for Mr. Lazy. He went through all the trading places but, again, Mr. Lazy was nowhere to be seen. Unable to give Mr. Lazy the money in the form of a big profit, he turned it over to the god of land for help.

Finally, the god of land located Mr. Lazy in his home and he devised a scheme to hand the money over. He left the money in the backyard, and then tried to get Mr. Lazy to do some gardening and therefore find the money. But, Mr. Lazy was too lazy even to clean up his own backyard, and so the money was still lying in the backyard untouched.

Upon reading the report, the lord of death told Mr. Lazy: "Sorry, you were actually given lots of wealth during your life time. But you did not make any effort to get it. Case dismissed!"

(This story is an adaptation from a Buddhist folk tale at *www. thegardenofwisdom.com/1/.../mr-lazy-a-buddhist-folk-story.ht)*

LESSONS LEARNT

Laziness does not pay. To be able to prosper one must be energetic and spent the energy for a good course. The land can be the source of all riches if energy is spent tilling it.

From a Rich Man's Son to a Beggar

On one of my routine outings I (Prof. Bwisa) was taking a beer from my favourite joint. There were several reasons that made me make the joint my favourite. One was that it was close to my residence, the other was that it was a "cool" place, another was that my "buddies" frequented it hence it provided an ideal networking venue for me. But above all it belonged to a rich and famous individual who died in the mid-1970s.

On this day as I was just about to leave having taken my normal 3 beers, two colleagues offered me a beer each. Turning the offer down would have been "anti-African" and looked rude but taking more would have broken my drinking principles. In this dilemma I accepted the offer but waited for an opportune time to ask the attendants to keep it for me until the next visit.

Meanwhile a young man had engaged me in a dialogue and I had just discovered that he was the son of the owner of the joint who had passed on. My assumption was that the young man was supervising his own business having inherited it from his father and the Asian I had noticed at the joint was the employed manager.

I discovered from the attendants and revellers that the young man's father owned the joint and was very rich, but the son could not manage the joint and always depended on the father when he was alive for handouts and had never taken the initiative to run the business.

When I finally got the opportunity to ask the attendants to keep my two beers, the young man, who overheard me, begged that I give him the two beers. I did not believe my ears and that made me do a little bit of investigative enquiries. I discovered from the attendants and revelers that the young man's was the original owner of the hotel and but had always depended on the father for hand-outs and never taken the initiative to run the business. Currently he had leased it out to the Asian. The young man was constantly broke and kept asking revellers for hand-outs – a habit that had never left him.

REFLECTION QUESTIONS

1. Why do you think Agriculture is said to be the back bone of the economy of many countries in Africa?

2. How early do you think a kiosk owner who makes breakfast for people going to work and supper for people after work wake up and how late does he/she go to sleep? Is this story relevant to such a kiosk owner?

3. Explain why Mr. Lazy man was not able to find the reaches in his backyard?

4. What actions would you have taken if you were Mr. Lazy man after the promise made to you did not become a reality?

CHAPTER TEN

ENTREPRENEURS PLANNING

THE ORPHAN BOY WHO BECAME VERY RICH

- *"Eshilahwa nishi" (Nothing lasts forever) African Proverb.*

Orphan Boy in Lakeside Community

Once upon a time there lived an orphan boy among a lakeside community. The community survived by fishing and the normal practice was not to fish from 11 am to 5 pm due to the belief that those were evil hours. For one it would be too hot and the belief was that by that time the fish would have fed and satisfied so none would be attracted to the fishermen's hooks and baits. They all preferred to wake up at 5 a.m. and fish until 8-9 a.m. or fish after midnight until 6-7 a.m. The orphan boy who had no fishing rods of his own would only wait till others were not using theirs for him to lease and go out into the lake during the hours believed by everybody to be bad. Of course nobody could refuse to give him a rod because they all believed he would catch nothing and even if he did they would only benefit from the fee they would receive from him.

The boy would go out alone and unknown to the community he would catch a lot of fish which he quietly and secretly sold to fishmongers and invested his profits in a faraway village. His investments multiplied manifold and he became very rich. Eventually he decided to transfer his riches from the far off village back to his own community. While there were those who thought he must have stolen that wealth others thought he was simply a very lucky person. He married a beautiful hardworking girl and they lived well thereafter.

LESSON

Planning: Here we learn that even without physical resources of your own good planning can be the key to success. First the boy planned how to benefit from the community even if he had no resources. He then planned well how to invest his profits.

Another lesson we learn is that the people of the boy's community did not understand that when the boy was fishing alone during the hours which everybody superstitiously believed were bad there was no competition. The only hooks in the sea were the boy's. It was not easy for the boy to stand under the hot sun during those hours, but he endured and caught fish.

So... if you want to make the difference spot what other people do not do because they cannot bear with the obstacles, the load of work, the timing... And then act. Two - spot what other people have not done yet, because they think there is no market. And then target that market... And above all: Do what you Love - but do it.

The Greedy Hyena

Once upon a time there lived a hyena. Mr. Hyena was known in the entire village for his greed. He simply could not say no to food no matter how much he had eaten. He could eat and eat until his stomach could take no more forcing him to vomit.

One day on his way to a far off village for the harvesting ceremony he found the path on which he walked on split to two paths leading to different directions. What was more confusing for the hyena was that the aroma of delicious food seemed to be coming from both directions. After much thought he decided to take one path but after a few steps he decided to take the next. This went on for some time until he finally decided to have one foot on one path and the next one the other.

Slowly and salivating at the thought of how much food he was going to eat he walked on. Soon his feet could part no more but he forced them to until his body tore suddenly into two. He fell down and bled to death.

LESSON

The key lesson we learn here is one of nurturing quality: Willing to take charge of, and watch over a venture until it can stand alone. Successful entrepreneurs do nurture one venture until it is time to introduce another. They take one step at a time and avoid biting more than they can chew. Unplanned business expansion and/or diversification can be disastrous because the too many tasks involved can only wear out the entrepreneur's management efforts.

THE POOR MAN AND THE DRUM OF HONEY

THERE was once a Poor Man, who lived in a house next to a wealthy and kind Merchant who sold oil and honey. One day the merchant sympathized with the poor old man and gave him a drum of honey. The Poor Man was delighted, and thought he wanted to plan well how to use it. Meanwhile he put it carefully away on the top shelf. One evening, as he was gazing at it, he started saying to himself,—

"I wonder how much honey there is in that drum. There is a large quantity. If I should sell it, I could buy some cattle and sheep and goats. Every year I should have calves, and before long I should own a big herd of animals. Then I should sell some of the animals and be rich enough to marry a wife. Perhaps we might have a son. And what a fine boy he would be! So tall, strong, and obedient! But if he should disobey me," and he raised the walking stick which he held in his hand, "I should punish him like this!" and he swung the stick over his head and brought it heavily to the ground, knocking, as he did so, the drum off the shelf so that the honey ran over him from head to foot and on to the ground. All he could do was lick the little that was on his body but the rest disappeared in the soil.

LESSON

Never plan too much ahead, better still do not count your chicks before they hatch or never dance yourself lame before the real dance.

THE JACKAL AND THE WOLF

ONCE upon a time a Jackal, who lived near a road to the sea, saw a wagon returning from the seaside laden with fish. He tried to get into the wagon from behind, but he could not. He then ran through the bush ahead of the wagon without being seen and lay in the road as if dead. The wagon came up to him, and the driver cried to the owner, "Here is a fine skin-cloth for your wife!"

"Throw it into the wagon," said the owner, and Jackal was thrown in.

The wagon traveled on, and all the while Jackal was throwing out the fish into the road; he then jumped out himself and started feasting on the fish. But alas! The jackal noticed an old Wolf coming along the road and eating the fish the jackal had thrown out. The jackal was extremely annoyed and quickly thought out a punishment for the wolf, "You can get plenty of fish, too, if you lie in the way of a wagon as I did, and keep quite and see whatever happens."

"So!" mumbled Wolf.

Accordingly, when the next wagon came from the sea, Wolf stretched himself out on the road.

"What ugly thing is this?" cried the driver when he saw the wolf. He took a stick and thrashed the wolf. All the time the wolf, according to the instructions of the jackal, lay quiet as he was being beaten. Satisfied that he had beaten the wolf well the driver continued on his journey leaving the wolf for dead. Eventually the Wolf got up and went off to tell his misfortune to Jackal, who pretended to comfort him.

LESSONS LEARNT

Do not reap where you never sowed. Plan for your own destiny. In entrepreneurship those who go into business on a me-too syndrome i.e. by merely aping others already in business do not succeed.

Minting Money from Linkages

Early in the 1990s I (professor Bwisa) bought a plot in Nairobi and started building my residential house. I chose to use natural stone and sand as my main building materials. One day as I was supervising the building activities, a well-dressed young man came to the site and claimed that the stones and sand I was using were not the best. He said it so sarcastically that I also decided to be sarcastic in my reply to him, "If you can deliver better material then, I will buy them at Ksh.1000 more than I am buying them now." A deal was made. The young man said he was not going to take any money upfront but will come back in six hours given that he had to fetch the stones from afar. He even assured me that should I not like the stones he would bring, I was under no obligation to buy the stones.

In six hours, the young man returned sitting in a cabin of a lorry ferrying the promised building stones. Meanwhile, I had summoned stone assessors to be on standby to advise me on the quality of the stones. After thorough scrutiny and inspection of the stones I was advised that they were the best stones for construction. I not only kept my promise but also enlisted the young man as my supplier for the rest of the materials. I also recommended him to my colleagues who were constructing their houses.

Close to ten years after I had completed building my house and was comfortably residing in it, I received a visitor who turned out to be the same young man whom I had enlisted as my supplier of building stones. The visitor's revelation was that at the time he was supplying the building materials he was only a link man – a broker. He could go to building sites and promise to deliver the best materials. After obtaining the order, he would go to where the lorries with building materials were packed waiting for buyers and select the best for delivery. He would negotiate prices with the actual material sellers and pick only those whose prices would earn him a good commission. From being a stone broker, he now owned a fleet of lorries. He thanked me for having recommended him to my friends and gave a present, which had been his main reason for visiting. Clearly, through sound planning, this young man had transformed his situation from being poor to becoming rich.

REFLECTION QUESTIONS

1. Using the story of the orphan boy discuss the debate that entrepreneurs are born and not made.

2. There are people who believe that everything that happens on earth is God's plan, therefore we do not have to waste time on planning for ourselves. Discuss this school of thought.

3. While planning for everything we do is important, discuss the main limitations of planning.

4. The community where the orphan boy believed that fish could not be caught during the day, why do you think the orphan boy was able to catch fish contrary to the superstition?

CHAPTER ELEVEN

EntrepReneurs
Results-Oriented

- *Obiala akakesanga (he who plants will harvest) African Proverb*

A FARMER'S DAUGHTER

Once upon a time a farmer sent his daughter to sell milk in town. As she balanced the pail of milk on her head and walked to town she started day dreaming. Very many thoughts ran through her head, "The milk in this pail will provide me with cream, which I will make into butter, which I will sell in the market, and buy a dozen eggs, which will hatch into chickens, which will lay more eggs, and soon I shall have a large poultry yard. I'll sell some of the fowls and buy myself a handsome new dress that I will wear and attract many young men and when they approach me for friendship, I'll toss my head like this and pass them by." As the girl tossed her head the pail of milk lost balance and fell spilling all the milk.

LESSON LEARNED

The girl was result-oriented. She had good plans for her future but alas! They were one too many a plan. It is good to have few manageable plans.

MY NIECE

My nephew graduated from university with "flying colours" and applied to work in one of the best paying banks in the country. She sat for the interview and passed and was told to report in three months. The offer was a position with a high-paying salary. Excited and looking for a bright future, and even before she reported to work, she used her little savings and borrowed from friends and immediately bought a car on hire purchase believing that with the high salary she would comfortable mange the installments. Unfortunately the bank collapsed just when she was supposed to report. Yes – she was results – oriented but had "counted her chickens before they hatched".

REFLECTION QUESTIONS

1. There are people who believe that nothing really happens as planned. So there is no need to plan. Discuss this.

2. Do you think that the girl's dreams were realistic? Can one grow rich just by selling butter from milk cream?

CHAPTER TWELVE

ENTREPR**E**NEURS
Efficiency-oriented

The Trumpeter

- *Sititi silemia mwoyo (little drops of water will quench the thirst or desire)*

THE HORN BLOWER

There once lived a horn blower. He was caught by the enemy one day. He cried out to his captors, "Please do not kill me. Besides blowing the horn, I do nothing else, I do not kill." The enemy replied, " That's why you must die. Though you do not fight, your efficient and effective horn blowing stirs all the others to battle."

LESSON LEARNED

Efficiency does not necessarily lie in big numbers and a team is as efficient as each of its members.

THE BOY AND THE JAR OF GROUNDNUTS

A boy put his hand into a jar of groundnuts and grasped as many as his fist could possibly hold. But when he tried to pull it out again, he found he couldn't do so, for the neck of the jar was too small to allow the passage of so large a handful. Unwilling to lose his nuts but unable to withdraw his hand, he burst into tears.

A bystander, who saw where the trouble lay, said to him, "Come, my boy, don't be so greedy. Be content with half the amount, and you'll be able to get your hand out without difficulty."

LESSON LEARNED

Do not attempt to do too much at once. Be efficient by using little by little.

Holding Cash in Stock

A *Jua Kali* (informal) furniture maker in my (prof. Bwisa) estate landed a lucrative ART (African Retail Traders) order but realized he had no funds to fulfill the order. He therefore approached a micro finance institution for a loan. I was asked to evaluate the risk of lending to this entrepreneur. My visit to the entrepreneur revealed that the entrepreneur had recently bought lots of timber – more than he currently needed - and stored it in a makeshift structure. The reason he had bought that much was because the government had waged war on illegal timber yards and many of them were selling their timber off at throw-away prices and closing. To the entrepreneur this was a chance he would not wish to let go hence had used all his funds to stock timber that he did not need immediately. Storing in a makeshift structure posed the risk of the timber getting spoilt even before it was used.

My advice to the micro finance institution was that the entrepreneur did not need the loan. He could convert the excess timber into cash.

REFLECTION QUESTIONS

1. What in your opinion does the phrase "too much of something is poisonous" mean?

2. Discuss circumstances when few is better than more

CHAPTER THIRTEEN

ENTREPRE**N**EURS
Have **N**-arch

- *Oenja anyolanga (he who seeks finds) African Proverb*

THE MEETING OF ANIMALS WITH HORNS

Once upon a time all horned animals decided to call a meeting to be attended only by the animals with horns. The hare being an animal without horns but who had a burning desire to attend the meeting thought hard. To be able to attend the meeting, the hare resolved to make himself horns made of clay wax.

At the appointed time the hare adorned itself with the horns made of wax. All the other horned animals also came. The meeting progressed well but took quite some time. The sun as usual started getting hotter and hotter as the meeting was being held in the open. As the meeting progressed the hare realized that with the sun getting hotter and hotter his horns would melt and hence its true identity would be known. The hare therefore, asked the buffalo who was chairing the meeting to finish the agenda of the meeting, as it had some pressing issues to attend to. The buffalo nevertheless did not see urgency of the hare's request. The hare on realizing that its trick of having fake horns was going to be discovered decided to rush out of the meeting before it was concluded. He decided never to try such a trick as there was the likelihood of having been killed by the horned animals if they would have found out that the hare's horns were not real as per the requirement of the meeting.

LESSON

The first lesson is that where there is a will there is a way. If you really want something even if it is risky you can get it if you plan well. But there must be a burning desire in you to get it.

Entrepreneurship exists under condition of risk and uncertainty. Risk refers to the variability of outcomes (returns). If there is not risk the returns are certain. A firm operating in risk free environment would continue to expand forever, since a negative outcome could not occur. Therefore, risk is a limit to the ever-expanding entrepreneurship. Uncertainty refers to the confidence entrepreneurs have in their estimates of how the world works. Their understanding of causes and effects in the environment is clear. The story of the hare attending the meeting of animals with horns when in fact it did not have horns can be used to illustrate the two entrepreneur characteristic of risk and uncertainty.

Scraping Fortune out of Scrap Metal

For over a period 100 years there was a one dominant player in the field of selling weighing machines on the Kenyan market - Avery India Limited. The company had been supplying weighing machines and weighing automation solutions to customers since 1911. So when in 2008 there appeared a new type of weighing machines by the brand name Zing effectively competing Avery, the first author of this book was curious to trace its emergency. Judging from the name he had actually concluded that the Chinese were now giving old timers a run for their money. He was wrong. It was a young Kenyan called Clement Wainaina who had introduced the new weighing machines.

When Clement graduated from Kenya's prestigious Kenyatta University he wasted no time looking for wage employment. This is what virtually every Kenyan (and indeed African) graduates would do given that in Kenya (and by extension in Africa) parents take children to school (or people go to school) with the single objective of getting a good white collar job on graduation. Self-employment as an alternative career option has not yet been well embraced in the continent's educational policy and philosophy.

When Clement took up a teaching post in Kenya's capital city of Nairobi his dream was to make a fortune. Alas! His "get-rich-in-wage-employment" dream was never to be.

Faced with a litany of problems working for an employer and after an extended period of soul searching, Clement took the bold step and resigned from his job, not necessarily knowing where he would earn his keep from next and armed only with the optimism of the success of the technological gamble that he was determined to convert into a business start-up.

From knowledge acquired during the three-year Bachelor of Science degree course at Kenyatta University coupled by observations at metal foundries, and perhaps without warning propelled by the saying that necessity is the mother of invention, Clement put in place a simple smelting process by vaporizing paraffin using an old stove to create the necessary pressure and high temperatures. For casting the melted scrap metal, he improvised using molasses and sand. This was in 1994 at a Nairobi's Light industries area.

His first rental premises served both as the foundry and business premises. It was a see-through temporary wooden structure for which he paid rent of Kshs 200 ($2.5 US dollars then) per month.

Entrepreneurship theory teaches that one of the distinguishing factors for most start-ups is that the proprietor has to work extremely long hours. This was the case with Wainaina. Right from the start and for the days that followed, Clement worked day and night smelting the weighing scale clips. The people who might have wanted to steal from him at night were apparently scared by the fierce, hissing flame that emanated from the intensifier.

The initial raw material investment was two kilogrammes of scrap metal. He made 20 pieces of weighing machine clips which he sold at Kshs. 40 ($.50 then). Within three months, he had started branching into the making of other parts of weighing scales.

He had to recoup all the profits into the business because his start-up capital was extremely low. All the resources that he used to start this business were from his meager terminal benefits he had received from his previous employer. He could not borrow from commercial banks since he did not have any asset that he could put up as collateral.

Ten years after starting, Wainaina formed Zing Engineering Works, a fully-fledged manufacturing concern boasting of more than 20 full time employees departmentalized into a workshop, foundry and show room.

His initial experience was that the smelting process was energy-intensive. When he moved from his initial temporary structure to the current premises, he decided to enter into partnership with a group of people who were looking for odd jobs within this area.

His partnership approach was designed on franchise principles. Thus he put together all the instruments, gadgets and the works that were necessary for setting up a foundry and then handed over the foundry to the young men. He trained the first three youths. He often held meetings with his partners and explained to them that there was need for them to run the foundry like it was their own asset and that he would be placing orders for various metallic parts and then paying for each item that they produced.

Similarly, at the workshop, Clement trained the first technician on how to use machines such as the lathe machine and the threading machine. Subsequently, the technician who was trained first started training other employees.

Clement Wainaina's was a road of incremental development. He started producing weighing machine parts. He then moved into his first brand of fully fledged weighing machines (which he named ZING) used for weighing off-counter items such as meat, sugar, flour and others. He then developed other brands of the same machine before he added to his production list platform-weighing machines that can weigh sacks of grains and other heavy items.

Thus in just three years Zing Engineering Works weighing machines had four brands, Zing I, Zing II, Zing Extra and Zing Platform, all of them being distinctly different in size and attuned for use in heavier material. Zing I is used for weighing up to 10 kilogrammes, Zing II items of 15 kilogrammes, Zing III for over 20 kilogrammes and Zing Platform for much heavier items of up to 250 kilogrammes such as maize and wheat sacks.

WHY THE NAME ZING?

Clement learned the consumers behaviors and discovered that many of them liked products manufactured out of the country. If he had used his last name - Wainaina- he would not have sold the weighing machines since many people think locally manufactured goods are of low quality. Zing, for him sounded Chinese and was meant to attract Kenyan customers who have over a long period of time, shown proclivity to Chinese products. This unique and Chinese name worked for his weighing machines.

GUERILLA MARKETING

When Wainaina went into the weighing machines business, little did he know that marketing would be a herculean task. He therefore did not limit his innovations to hardware technology. Once his gamble had paid off and he was able to produce as many as 20 weighing machines per month, the next significant challenge became marketing. The main concern was that potential customers were shop owners in the city's Central Business District, who were used to procuring weighing machines from well-established weighing machine manufacturers and /or from abroad. With no money to advertise, promote or hire a sales team penetrating the market that was tightly controlled by the well-established, large scale weighing machine producers such as AVERY, he faced a David and Goliath affair.

He started a shop to shop campaign marketing his products. This was mainly to shops owned by Asian traders who are known for their no-nonsense approach to business. His strategy was to dress up as smartly as possible, put the best weighing machine in a carton box and leave for town with his wife using public transport. He would leave his wife at a short distance from the shop he was going to visit. Then he would majestically walk into the targeted shop and proceed to entice the potential customer. Invariably, he would be asked to present one weighing machine. He would then walk to where his wife would be with the weighing machine and carry it to the shop. The idea was to have the shopkeeper imagine that he had come with a delivery car, which he had packed at a distance. This would increase the positive impression created and enhance his image as a serious entrepreneur who had a delivery vehicle when the reality was that he would have used public transport.

After having made a breakthrough with a sizeable number of Asian shop owners, Wainaina approached supermarkets, interestingly also owned by investors of Asian descent. From the initial pessimism about the marketability of the weighing machines, Wainaina's *N-arching* and strong desire to succeed has led to the name recognition of his products. With confidence built over time, the supermarkets now make frequent orders from him rather than him approaching them. His business has expanded and now attracts many customers.

UNLIMITED DIVERSIFICATION OR HYPER INNOVATION?

Wainaina hates waste. Using what would otherwise pass as waste material he did not limit himself to the manufacture of weighing machines, scales and spring balances. In fact, a visit to his workshop revealed that he had hundreds of products of all sizes all over the place. Many of the products that he had made were as a result of research by observing products already in the market. Other products were straight from his imagination.

One product that is now very popular in the market is the potato chipper. He observed people at some fish and chips shops chopping potatoes with knives. At other fish and chips restaurants, he saw that they were using imported potato chipping machines. He realized that he could use alternative materials to make similar potato chipping machines and sell to the restaurants. This worked and soon many fish and chips restaurants were placing orders with him. The potato chippers that he makes are a lot cheaper because he uses local material and he does not have to pay import duty like the imported ones.

At his local church, Wainaina realized that candles were lit and placed on windows and on tables. Seeing this, he had a brainwave. Why not develop candleholders in which the candles could be placed such that the wax would not pour on the church furniture and windows? This he reckoned would add aesthetics to the candle lighting tradition and practice in churches and reduce the dirt that accumulated from the burning of the candles and also reduce the danger of fires in the churches. Further, the churches he visited all used small candles and by making huge candleholders, he would encourage the church administrations to buy bigger candles that would burn for longer periods of time. He also made the bases of the candleholders with rubber to avoid scratching of the church furniture where they would be placed.

As already mentioned, the Zing Engineering Works workshop has many products. But much as there are hundreds of big and small items and gadgets that are a testimony to Wainaina's creativity, the thinking that went into their production is the same: fulfilling unmet needs and filling existing entrepreneurial gaps.

For instance, when he learned that chalk dusters were being imported from India at Kshs90 (about 1.25 US dollars) per piece, he realized that he could make the same chalk dusters and sell them at Kshs30 (about 0.4 US dollars) and still make a profit.

When he inquired and was told that paper spikes were imported rather than locally produced, he went into an overdrive calibrating metallic strips and making the selfsame paper spikes at his workshop.

Other products that have hit the market from Zing Engineering Works include toothpick holders, targeting the big hotels in Nairobi, roofing washers, rubber chair bases, toy cars, plastic mobile phone holders and weight lifting gear, and electric grain (maize) miller.

REFLECTION QUESTIONS

1. There is a feeling among some people that some ethnic groups in Africa risk more than others and are therefore more entrepreneurial than others. Discuss this.
2. The English people say that necessity is the mother of invention. Discuss this.

CHAPTER FOURTEEN

ENTREPREN**E**URS **E**NDURING

- *"Emiandu neliime" (Riches are like dew that can easily vanish). African proverb.*
- *Baada ya dhiki, faraja (Swahili). After hardship comes relief (English).*

THE PEASANTS AND A BARREL OF WINE

A long time ago two poor peasants were asked to haul a barrel of wine to a rich man to be paid handsomely. It was a hot day and they became so thirsty that they could not endure it any longer as the wine tempted them more and more. At last one of them, after long thought, said, "It will be all right if I pay for the drink." He took a sip, and handed his companion a coin. After a while the other peasant who had been paid could also not endure any longer and did the very same, took a sip of the wine and handed back the coin he had just been given. Back and forth they passed the coin, getting tipsier and tipsier, until the barrel was empty.

As you may have guessed they were made to pay for the wine by working on the vineyard for free for a long time.

LESSONS LEARNED

Patience and endurance pays. Many business people mistake cash for profit and keep withdrawing it from the business. They do not endure to wait until the business breaks even. They end up in debts they are not able to pay and their businesses go under.

THE FARMER AND HIS SONS

A farmer, at the point of death, wished to show his sons the secret to successful farming. He gathered his sons round him and said, "My sons, I am about to leave this world. All that I've left for you can be found in the vineyard. Dig, and you will find the hidden treasures."

As soon as the old man was dead, the sons labored, digging in the vineyard. They turned over the soil again and again, but could find no treasure. However, the vines were strengthened and improved by this thorough tillage. The grapes that emerged were big and juicy, and produced the best vintage ever. This more than repaid the brothers for all their hard work.

LESSONS LEARNED

Fortune does not come by itself. Hard work and endurance pays. Industry in itself is a treasure.

From Two Hens to a Billionaire

In the year 2010 Kenya lost a man who had literary walked the road of, "from rags to riches". His story was flashed all over by both the print and electronic media. His eulogy told of a man who had business endurance.

In 1932 in Kanyariri village, Kikuyu Division of Kiambu District Nelson Muguku was born in a family of an enterprising father. Young Muguku was eager for education but he only completed primary school education (then Junior Secondary) before his dream to pursue high school was frustrated by colonialists after his parents had convinced him to repeat the Kenya African Preliminary Examination at Kabete Intermediate School. "He repeated but when the results came out, he had done so well that the colonial administration cancelled the results. The argument was that Muguku, an African, must have cheated at the examination to pass so well. He was advised to go to Thika to learn carpentry instead - narratives have it.

Young Muguku obeyed his masters and joined Thika Technical School from 1950 to 1953 for a career in carpentry. He was to prove the colonialists wrong. He completed the four-year course in two years and soon afterwards, became an untrained teacher at Kapenguria Intermediate School in 1954 before being transferred to Kabianga Teachers' College (now Kabianga High School).

During his teaching period at Kabianga he had a hobby of keeping chicken. Muguku started with two chickens and a cock that he reared at a corner of his house. The school's principal requested Muguku if he could bring some eggs for his hens to sit on. This was on condition that when they hatched they would share the chicks. Muguku agreed to the boss and the principal brought in 13 eggs. Fortunately, all the eggs hatched and after the chicks matured, the principal took his share, but selected all the hens leaving Muguku with cocks only, which Muguku considered a raw deal but could not complain. Fortunately a month later, the principal was transferred, leaving behind six hens and a Cock. The principal's successor asked Muguku to buy and take control of the strolling hens, left by the former principal. His conditions were that Muguku would pay by giving him eggs in return.

They agreed for Muguku to buy each chicken at Ksh 15. He was to supply eggs at a rate of 25 cents each to pay the debt since he did not have cash to pay. Luckily, Muguku paid for the chicken in a record two months though he had thought it would take a year.

Impressed by the rate of return, he started toying with the idea of going into the poultry business. However, on mentioning this to his father who had tried poultry farming and lost all his 200 birds in an epidemic, the father discouraged him but Muguku's desire and resolve never waned.

Having emerged the best pupil and with his teaching experience in carpentry, Muguku started convincing himself that the title of an untrained teacher he was holding was an inappropriate title for him. Furthermore, in 1957, he stumbled on his younger brother's pay slip and could not believe that the brother, who did two years carpentry training and proceeded for teaching profession was earning Ksh. 350 against his own salary of Ksh. 280. Muguku quit teaching after feeling he was not getting enough and his efforts to improve his grade were being frustrated by the colonialists. "He had done all the exams and passed but they could not promote him, saying Africans could not go beyond certain grades,"his brother was heard narrating. Muguku severally applied for promotion but could not get one. He decided to quit wage employment.

With only two hens, a cock, a bicycle, few furniture and Sh 2,000 in his pocket and against the wishes of his parents and school principal, Nelson Muguku quit teaching in 1957 to venture into poultry business. He used the capital to buy the chickens and also to build a chicken coop and feed them for the first few days. It was not an easy venture. He supplied eggs for ten years then ventured into hatching chicks to supply other poultry farms. In 1963 his wife quit teaching to join him in the business. As his business grew, Muguku acquired a 22-acre farm for Ksh 100,000 and started a hatchery with a 9,000-egg incubator.

By 1972, demand for chicks had increased forcing Muguku to buy a new hatchery with a capacity of 42, 000 eggs a week. Muguku quickly discovered that egg-hatching was more profitable than egg-trading. However, the cost of input in the former is high. For instance, it requires one to have a stand-by generator and the chicks need tender care. Layers, on the other hand, do not require much attention.

Guided by the wisdom of, "do not put all your eggs in one basket", Muguku decided to run both lines.

Muguku was the first African in commercial poultry farming in Kenya for a good period of time but due to increasing demand for poultry products competition became inevitable and Muguku welcomed it. His philosophy was, "it is better to try and fail than fail to try".

From a humble beginning of owning a bicycle as the most valuable asset in late 1950s, Mr Muguku died as the biggest individual shareholder of Equity Bank which he joined when it was a building society close to 20 years earlier.

For Nelson Muguku it all started as a hobby. At his death in 2010 Muguku owned and ran Muguku Poultry Farm in Kikuyu, Kiambu, estimated to be worth more than Ksh 3 billion. At his death it was one of the largest hatcheries in the country with a capacity to hatch some 200,000 chicks per day. Besides, Muguku was the largest individual shareholder in Equity Bank holding 7,515,085 shares accounting 8.3 per cent of the bank's stake. The only other largest shareholder in the bank was British Investment Company (Britak) Limited, which is an institution.

REFLECTION QUESTIONS

1. Using the story of the farmer and his sons discuss how people in Africa can make wealth from their Agricultural land.

2. The climatic conditions are changing. These days there are longer spells of drought than rainy days meaning that harvests are getting far spaced. Discuss how farmers can endure these long spells of drought.

CHAPTER FIFTEEN

ENTREPRENE**U**RS
UNSTOPPABLE

- *"Eshianolie shikonanga shionyene" (What you will own, eat, possess, become is hidden). African proveb.*

- *"Amatsi keranga omwelema" (Even an expert swimmer can drown).* African proverb.

THE KING'S SON GETS MARRIED

Once upon a time a boy was born in a royal kingdom. He was a very handsome baby. As a prince the boy was to become king when his father died.

At the age of 7, the prince was very handsome and every girl wanted his hand in marriage. He also wanted to get married but not to a girl who wanted him for his fame and riches. He wanted to marry someone who really loved him.

"Dad," the prince said quietly. "I want to get married, I mean not in 15 years, I mean right now!"

"Don't you think you are a little too young to get married, son?"

"No!"

"If wishes were horses even beggars would ride, son. Wait ten years, and then you may get married."

"Okay, but do you promise?"

"Of course I do, when you are 17..."

Ten Years Later!!!!

"Well dad, I am now 17!" Said the prince.

"I know, now let's find the most beautiful girl in the land!"

"Yeah, let's go!" They went searching to find someone who loved the prince for himself and someone he could love in return. They searched the whole land, but everyone wanted him only because he was wealthy and famous.

"This is useless son; nobody loves you for who you are."

"Tomorrow we will look again. I am determined to find someone for myself and not my riches."

"Okay tomorrow," the tired king said while yawning. But remember, if wishes were horses ....

The next day they went searching again, but only in expensive houses. But all those people didn't like him. He almost gave up when he saw a little house he hadn't looked in yet. It had a beautiful garden with many nice flowers. He walked into the garden and saw a beautiful woman sitting on a bench embroidering something. Her eyes were as sweet as flowers. He then knew this would be the girl he would marry.

The garden was almost as beautiful as the girl. The garden looked as beautiful as the Prince's, only not quite as big.

"Hello, Miss," he said quietly. She turned and looked at him.

"Why are you here? Shouldn't you be in the palace?" she asked in a sweet, kind voice.

"I am looking for a woman to marry, and I saw you. My eyes grew wider," he said shyly.

"Thank you very much, your highness," she said in that same voice.

"What's your name?" he asked her.

"Nekesa," she whispered. "Will you marry me Nekesa?" he said in a brave, warrior- like voice.

"No, although you are handsome, good and kind and although I would love to be with you, your riches and wealth scare me."

The prince knew he had found who he was looking for, he persisted and pursued the girl with patience. After several months of courting they got married.

LESSON

You can get what you really want in life but, you must learn to try and try, you will succeed at last. Entrepreneurs are unstoppable. If they fail once they try again.

From Watching Trees to "Growing Money on Trees"

Not long ago I (Prof. Bwisa) decided to landscape my residence with beautiful plants. I had no problem finding where to buy the plants for on Thika Highway along which I drive on daily basis there is a lady who tends to a large variety of plants. While at her garden to buy the plants I engaged her in a dialogue.

She told me that only a year ago, she had been wondering what she was going to do with her life having been fired several times by her employers where she was working as a house help. Opportunities were hard to come by and she was starting to feel a little desperate when she recalled how her employers would every now and then, bring home plants for their garden boys to plant. There she saw her opportunity. She started breeding plants along the road and as she puts it the rest is history.

The young lady sells anything from ground cover flowers to palm trees to versed plants. She is not only a very busy lady, she is also doing relatively well.

"Mine is a very delicate business that demands total focus, lots of hard work and creativity," she told me. She has employed four other girls two of who chat to and attract drive-by customers while the other two prepare the nurseries for new seedlings. She does the selling herself.

"I have discovered that plants are like babies; they are alive and need nurturing to thrive. I am no different from a nursery school teacher who prepares children for higher education; we both have to put in serious effort, time and resources to achieve the final purpose." She told me

The lady told me that in the beginning she used to get it all wrong for she used to aim at matching what the other business people in the business were doing. She would spy nurseries in other places and then copy them. That did not give her the success that they had and that became her biggest entrepreneurship lesson. She thinks that most people are failing for being copycats and not letting their own identities reflect on their business. "If you see somebody selling brew and making a lot of money from it, do not go ahead and open a similar business next door. You will fail because you are offering nothing different and because your competitor may have some brewing abilities you cannot have."

This realization made the lady change accordingly and the sheer size and variety of her yard tells a story of a lady in command of her trade.

I was informed that from a humble investment of less than Sh 5,000, the business is now worth in excess of Sh2 million. Besides plants, the lady has diversified into the sale of vases and manure.

Plants sell from Ksh. 30 to Ksh. 250 making an average price of Ksh. 140. An average of three customers visit the business on daily basis buying an average of 5 plants and the business is open 7 days a week. This works out at Ksh. 63000 per month or an equivalent of a lecturer's salary. Indeed there are varieties that sell at Ksh. 15 000 a seedling and on a good day she can sell a dozen of them.

The lady is convinced that entrepreneurs should not shy away from attempting the impossible just because they have no academic training. With a burning passion to excel, nothing is impossible, so she believes and adds that the trick of a successful plants business is variety.

Her advice to young people was that they quit making excuses and adds that lack of formal education is not a lack of practical education. The world is full of opportunities and all we have to do is to be open-minded.

REFLECTION QUESTIONS

1. It is often said that patience pays. Discuss situations you have experienced that proof this saying.

2. The Swahili say that, **"kuteleza sio kuanguga"** meaning a slip is not a fall. Discuss this saying.

CHAPTER SIXTEEN

ENTREPRENEU**R**S
RESPONSIBLE

- *Eliobola nilio elikhuyala.* (What you say is what you will be judged by). African proverb.

- *Amasika shikenenera shiamwene* (Do not shade tears for what belongs to someone else). African proverb.

- *Amatsi kera omwilama.* (Even an expert swimmer can drown). African proverb.

THE TWO ORPHANS

Long time ago there were two orphans namely Mwambu and his sister Sela. Their parents died when they were very young and left them a big piece of land which had many cattle and goats. Mwambu worked on the farm looking after the herds of animals while Sela grew crops.

When Mwambu became a teenager, he loved to go to village dances where almost all the girls were attracted to him as he had grown into a handsome young man. Unfortunately he never took his sister with him.

One night after he left, Sela noticed three young men around their hut. She was frightened and begged Mwambu not to leave her alone in the night. He refused to listen. The three young men continued to spy on Sela and one night they broke into the hut where she was and threatened to kill her if she refused to go away with them.

Sela begged them to allow her to sing a bridal song before she left with them. The song was actually a song that was sang in a secret language that she and Mwambu had composed to call each other if either of them was in danger. When Sela sang, the brother heard her and responded by singing back and left the dance at once and ran home only to find Sela gone. He followed the footprints into the forest.

It was not long before he saw the figures of three men and the girl. The first man was pushing the girl through the forest as the others urged him to make her walk faster.

When Mwambu saw what was happening to the sister he was so angry that he flung his spear at the man who was nearest to him. When the other men realized what had happened to their colleague they fled through the forest leaving Sela alone.

After this incident Mwambu always took his sister to the dances with him. Here, Sela gradually met a young man who asked to marry her. Mwambu also met and fell in Love with one of the village girls.

The parents of Mwambu's bride agreed to organize a huge feast so that the two orphans could be married at the same ceremony. Mwambu gave his bride's parents many sheep and goats from his herds. Sela's husband built a nice new hut not far away. The two couples became good friends and worked together. They eventually created so much wealth that they were able to employ many young people in the village.

LESSON

The key entrepreneurship lesson we learn here is responsibility. Mwambu took it as his responsibility to save his sister after he refused to listen to her when danger was looming. Entrepreneurs always accept responsibility for their own actions rather than passing the buck like blaming it on the customer; they are morally, legally and mentally accountable for their ventures; they uphold business ethics.

Other lessons learned here include:

Partnerships: The orphans succeeded in running the enterprise as partners with each one of them having clearly defined duties/ roles. They later brought in their spouses and their enterprise flourished even more. Successful family businesses can best flourish if there is good division of labour with clearly demarcated duties and responsibilities.

THE MAGIC PEARL

Once upon a time, there was a goat, named Esolo, and his friend, Esangi, the antelope. They lived in a cave just outside a bamboo forest. One day, Esangi, the antelope, was out eating bamboo. Inside one of the pieces of bamboo he saw a very shiny, white object. He picked it up. He called his friend, Esolo, the goat, over to look at it.

Esolo said, "What in the world is that?" Suddenly there was a loud bang and the unusual object said, "I am a magical pearl and I will serve you at all times."

Esangi said, "If you are stolen will you serve the thief?" "No, I will not. You are my masters," the pearl said.

Esangi said, "So, you are magical?" "Of course," the pearl said. So they kept the pearl.

A few weeks later, the King of the jungle heard that Esangi and Esolo had discovered a magic pearl and were having great fortune. So, the king sent his guards to fetch the magical pearl and bring it back to him. One night the guards crept over to Esangi and Esolo's cave and stole the pearl.

The next morning Esangi and Esolo realized the pearl was missing and they were very upset. They looked all over for it. Then from afar they saw the king's workers loading his luggage and the pearl into a boat to take to his private palace. The king was on the boat when the pearl became red-hot, started to burn a hole in the boat, and caused the boat to sink.

When Esangi and Esolo found out what happened they rushed to the lake. As they got there the pearl rose up from the water and said, "If I can't be with my real masters, I will not help anyone at all."

As it said that it shot into the sky and became what is now known as the wishing star. Later, the pearl decided that it would grant everyone's wish except for greedy people like the King.

LESSON

The moral of this tale is: irresponsible behaviour and greed will get you nowhere in life. Entrepreneurs do not steal to get rich.

Making Money on Two Wheels

Sometimes in the beginning of the 2000 decade the concept of Structural Adjustment Programmes (SAPs) reached Kenya. The government decided to retrench certain categories of civil servants. These included young men and women who had been employed as clerks and messengers earning on the average Ksh. 10 000 per month. The idea was to give them Ksh. 40 000 as a send-off. It was decided that before they are retrenched they would be trained in how to invest their retrenchment money. I was selected to be one of the trainers and given a group to train.

As you may have guessed correctly, every retrenchee thought Kshs. 40,000 was too little to start a business. This prompted me to undertake research to see what ksh. 40,000 could do. At that time the concept of **boda boda** (bicycle shuttle transport) was just picking up in Kenya and particularly in Western Kenya. One of the authors observed that the **boda boda** operators made as a minimum Ksh. 200 on a bad day otherwise they could make up to Ksh. 500 per day.

Armed with this information the author challenged some of his trainees to consider starting boda boda business. With Ksh. 40,000 they could buy 10 bicycles then. One could then keep them at home and employ young men who were idle and jobless to be coming every morning to take a bicycle and return it in the evening with only Ksh. 100. The prospect of making Kshs. 500 to give back only 100 would be attractive. In the first month the owner would collect Kshs. 1000 per day from ten bicycles this totaled to Ksh. 30,000 per month.

Out of the Kshs. 30,000 he would pay himself the 10,000 being his salary prior to retrenchment and maintain the status quo. He would set aside 5,000 for bicycle maintenance. He would deposit 5,000 in a bank and use 5,000 to improve his family's standard of living. He would then use 1,000 to thank himself for the work well done. The remaining 4,000 he would buy an extra bicycle so that in his second month he would get 33000 as opposed to 30,000 in the first month. In the third month he would add two bicycles to his old fleet. If you extrapolate this trend you will find that every month one could be adding to his fleet of bicycles and also increase his bank deposits. With good business planning he could make a substantive saving to qualify for a loan with which to graduate to a motorized transport system.

Just as the training was getting into gear political interference came in and the whole exercise was stopped by the government after it had been sued by one now late politician – Mr Kenndy Kiliku. The groups formed by the author insisted that he continues to train them and give them more practical and realistic examples of starting on a shoestring budget. That would have, however, been illegal. Eventually a deal was reached. The author would write business start-up articles and sell them to a newspaper and they would buy that newspaper and read them. That deal was eventually made with the Standard Newspaper. The author was allocated a Sunday column titled "Small business forum with professor Bwisa."

He ran the column between 2000 and 2002 and then discovered that while he was being paid an amount for the articles, the same articles were also being bought by regional media houses without any extra payment going to the author. This opened a new business opportunity, i.e. set up a website where the articles would be posted for sale.

This brought the author in contact with a young man who had just graduated from the university and was designing websites – a Mr. Phillip Nyamwaya who built the website www.professorbwisa.com.

After graduating from the Jomo Kenyatta University of Agriculture and Technology Phillip and a colleague set up intrepid (www.intrepidkenya.com.) and went on to win the Youth Entrepreneur of the year 2009 by Kenya Institute of Management – Annual Business. Intrepid Data Systems is an innovative enterprise productivity, mobile technology and digital branding firm which has been in operation since 2004.

Dialogue with Philip revealed that his desire to become an entrepreneur emerged towards his last 2 years in the university. He noted that the feeling that he is doing what he loves is his main entrepreneurial drive.

Phillip says that he grew up in a home where they were encouraged to excel and explore their gifts and talents. His parents did their best to see that he grew with opportunities around him. He further says that after his KCSE exam, he got a lot of good advice from older professionals regarding what career path to pursue in future.

Once in business Phillip, started dreaming and his biggest business dream is to grow and expand the business' range of services and reach out into the region. His advice to the Kenyan youth is fivefold:

- **One** - Surround yourself with persons who think positively and who would encourage you to (wisely) pursue your dream.

- **Two** - Start from where you are and with the resources you have.

- **Three** - Document your plan and get advice from professionals regarding aspects of your business where you may not have the necessary skills (e.g. compliance with the government regulation, Finance and Administration, Marketing).

- **Four** - Read and meditate on the lives and experiences of successful and (not-so-successful) entrepreneurs. Learn and apply as much as you can from their experiences.

- **Five** - Formalize your business entity as soon as possible. Quit hustling and regularize your business. This means you are serious about your business and what it stands for.

DISCUSSION QUESTIONS

1. Discuss ways in which pupils can be responsible for their education.

2. Discuss how responsible parents should bring up their children

3. Explain why Kings and rulers should not take other people's property by force without their permission.

CHAPTER SEVENTEEN

ENTREPRENEURS
Self-confident

- *"Eshimwelo shibula eshindi" (A basket begets another or success breeds success). African proverb.*

THE TIGER, THE RAM, AND THE JACKAL

Once upon a time, in the wilderness Mr. TIGER was returning home from hunting when he came across a kraal of Ram. Now, Mr. Tiger had never seen Ram before. He approached Mr. Ram submissively and said, "Good day, friend! What may your name be?" The other in his hoarse voice and thumbing his breast with his forefoot, said, "I am Ram and who are you?"

"Tiger, "answered the other, more dead than alive, and ran home as fast as he could. He went straight to Mr. Jackal who lived at the same place as him and told him, "Friend Jackal, I am quite out of breath, and am so frightened. I have just seen a terrible looking fellow, with a large and thick head, and on my asking him what his name was, he answered me proudly, "I am Ram."

"What a foolish fellow you are, "cried Jackal, "to let such a nice piece of steak stand! Why did you do so? Anyway show me tomorrow where this kraal is. Together we shall have a nice meal of Mr. Ram."

Next day the two set off early in the morning for the kraal of Ram, and as they approached at a distance, Ram, who was out grazing the soft morning grass saw them and immediately went to his wife and said, "I fear this is our last day, for Jackal and Tiger are both coming against us. "Take up the child in your arms and go out with it. When the two approach pinch it to make it cry as if it were hungry." Ram did so as the enemies came on.

Mr. Tiger who was still afraid of Ram was shivering walking behind Mr. Jackal. Jackal had known that Tiger would probably run away so he had tied Tiger to himself with a string so that he could not run away. Jackal kept urging Tiger, "Come on, let us go." When they were very near Mrs Ram pinched her child who started crying. At that time Mr. Ram said in a loud voice, "You have done well, Friend Jackal, to have brought us Tiger to eat, for you hear how my child is crying for food."

On these dreadful words Tiger, notwithstanding the encouragements from Jackal set off in full force and a great speed dragging Jackal after him over hill and valley, through bushes and over rocks, and never stopped to look behind him till he brought back himself and half-dead Jackal to his place again. And so Ram escaped.

LESSONS LEARNT

Confidence and courage are good things. It is the confidence and courage of the Ram and his wife that saved them. Self-confident entrepreneurs will try out businesses otherwise feared by others. Even in bad times confident entrepreneurs stick on with a belief that "to slip is not to fall."

REFLECTION QUESTIONS

1. Discuss ways in which people can build self-confidence.

2. Many students fail their examinations not because they are fools but because of lack of self-confidence – discuss this statement.

CHAPTER EIGHTEEN

ENTREPRENEURSHIP IN THE BIBLE

- *Wele khakaba anyala biosi* (God the almighty is mighty)

THE RICH MAN AND HIS THREE SERVANTS

There is a parable in the Bible about the rich man who was going on a long journey. He called his three servants together and told them they would be caretakers of his property while he was gone. He gave five talents to one servant, two to another, and one to the third—to each according to his ability. The master then left on his journey. The servants went forth into a world open to enterprise and investment. The servant who had received five talents went into business and made five more. The servant who received two made two more. But the servant who received one hid the master's property in a hole in the ground.

The master returned to settle his accounts. The servant who had received five talents came forth. "My lord," he said, "you entrusted me with five talents; see, I have made five more!" "Well done, good and faithful servant!" the master responded. "You have been faithful over a little, I will set you over much. Enter into the joy of your lord!" Then the servant who had been given two talents approached the master. "My lord," he said, "you entrusted me with two talents; see, I have made two talents more!" The master praised the servant in a like manner.

Then the one who had been given one talent approached his master. "My lord," he said, "I knew you to be a hard man; you reap where you have not sown, and gather where you have not scattered; and being afraid I went and hid your talent in the ground. See, you have what is yours!"

The master's response was swift and harsh: "You wicked and indolent slave! You were aware that I reap where I have not sown, and gather where I have not scattered; you ought for that reason to have invested my money with the bankers; then, on my return, I should have received my own with interest."

The master ordered that the talent be taken away from the lazy servant and given to the one with the ten talents. "For to everyone who possesses not," said the master, "even that which he has shall be taken away. Cast that useless slave into the outer darkness; there shall be weeping and the grinding of teeth!"

This is the bible Parable of the Talents (Matthew 25:14-30). This New Testament parable teaches us good entrepreneurship lessons. It is a story about capital, investment, entrepreneurship, and the proper use of scarce economic resources. The rich man is a venture capitalist and the servants are entrepreneurs and business people.

LESSONS

One lesson we learn is that hard work pays. Regardless of the initial capital, the two servants who worked hard to double what they were given were rewarded handsomely by the master. Thus, the amount of capital you start with is not a major determinant of your reward. You can indeed start a business without money by simply being creative and entrepreneurial. You begin with an idea which will mature into other forms of wealth. It is also what you do with the amount of money you have that matters not the amount itself.

Another lesson is that business failure is not necessarily the loss of capital, but a lack of effort to increase it or to add value to your business idea. The third servant did not increase the capital given to him hence was regarded a failure. Indeed, from an entrepreneurial perspective the difference between entrepreneurs and business people is that entrepreneurs are risk-lovers who yearn for and achieve business growth while business people are contented with what they have achieved and do not want to risk it by re-investing for growth. Thus, *all entrepreneurs are business people BUT not all business people are entrepreneurs.* The first two servants were entrepreneurs while the third one was a business person. The key entrepreneurial characteristics we filter from this parable are: Risk-taking, hardworking, high N-arc (need to achieve).

REFLECTION QUESTIONS

1. The bible has the following verses: Mathew 19:23 and Luke 18:23-24. It is hard for a rich man to enter the kingdom of heaven.... It is easier for a camel to go through the eye of a needle than for a rich man to enter the kingdom of heaven; MARK 10:23 How hard it is for the rich to enter the Kingdom of God. Discuss these verses in relation to entrepreneurship – do they discourage or encourage entrepreneurship? Why?

2. What would the third servant in the story above have done differently if he had asked the Lord what to do with the one talent?

ENTREPRENEURIAL LEARNING ACTIVITY

1. Identify two individuals in your community where you live who are successful entrepreneurs and contact them for the purpose of interviewing them. In your interview, seek answers to the following questions:

    *   How did they start their business enterprises?

    *   What initial preparation did they make before launching their businesses or careers?

    *   What do they find challenging in performing their work as entrepreneurs?

    *   What are the main benefits of being an entrepreneur?

    *   What advice do they have for you?

Bibliography

Ashlima, D. L. (2000). Otto Knoop, "Die drei Sprüche," Ostmärkische Sagen, Märchen und Erzählungen (Lissa: Oskar Eulitz' Verlag, 1909), 72, 147-149.

Ashmore, C. M. (1990). Entrepreneurship in vocational education. In C. A. Kent (Ed.). *Entrepreneurship Education: Current developments, future directions.* (pp.211-229). New York: Quorum Books.

BBC (2004). Profile: Bill Gates http://news.bbc.co.uk/2/hi/business/3428721.stm

Bandura, A. (1977). *Social learning theory.* New York: General Learning Pres.

Bwisa, H. M (1998). How to find and evaluate a business opportunity: A guide to those contemplating starting an own business. Mukmik consultants, Nairobi.

Bwisa, H. M. (1989) 'Scientific Co-operation for Development in Africa', African Development Review 2(1), June: 1-19.

Bwisa, H. M. (1991). "University-Government-Industry Linkages." In Agoki, Tsunoda, Makhanu and Mwatelah (eds). Technological Solutions for Economic Development in Kenya: Now and the 21st Century (pp 20 - 28). Nairobi, Kenya.

Bwisa, H. M. (2003) Alleviation Of Energy-Propelled Rural Poverty: An Entrepreneurial Approach. In Climate Network Africa - proceedings of the workshop on energy demand, CDM, Nepad and millennium development goals in east Africa. Hilton hotel — Nairobi, Kenya

Bwisa, H. M. (2003). Entrepreneurship education in Kenya: A reality or plodding on? International conference on Entrepreneurship development – USIU – Nairobi – Kenya

Bwisa, H. M. (2005). Should Entrepreneurs Advance the Profit-Maximization Objective? In Shareholder Value and the Common Good (Eds. David Lutz and Paul Mimbi. Strathmore university Press

Bwisa, H. M. (2007) Muko's dilemma: diversification, expansion, or other? A case study. Global Business School Network Africa

Bwisa, H. M. (2011). Entrepreneurship Theory and Practice: A Kenyan perspective. The Jomo Kenyatta Foundation.

Bwisa, H. M. Et al (1991). Final technical report on Industrial organization of Vegetable Oil Sector in Kenya. IDRC (Kenya).

Bwisa, H. M. et al (1998) A diagnostic study on cotton ginning and textiles industry development. Final report commissioned by the ministry of industrial development in collaboration with the ministry of planning and national development. African development and economic consultants ltd Nairobi – Kenya

Bwisa, H. M., (1998). Demand-driven micro and small enterprise research in Kenya: Critical issues. In International Labour Organization - ISEP - Geneva.

Bwisa, H. M., (2002) Factors that Kill Entrepreneurial Spirit. The Daily Nation, Nairobi, 4 August

Bwisa, H. M., (2005) – Small Business Development and Management for Private Animal Health Services Providers: A training manual. AU/IBAR. AU/IBAR, Nairobi

Bwisa, H. M., et al: (1999) information-based business development services in Kenya. Occasional paper no. 66, university of Nairobi, Institute for Development Studies (IDS)

Bwisa, H.M (2005). Bungoma the land of opportunity: An entrepreneurship and investment guide for Bungoma District. Mukmik Consultants, Nairobi.

Bwisa, H.M. (1996) 'An Inventory of Inventions and Innovations Originating from Publicly Funded Institutions of Research in Kenya'. African Technology Policy Studies Networl - Nairobi.

Bwisa, H.M. (2007) Tim Wanyonyi (a): does culture trigger entrepreneurship? A case study. Global Business School Network Africa

Bwisa, H.M.; Gacuhi, A. R. (1997) "Diffusion and Adaptation of Technology from research institutes and universities in Kenya: an empirical investigation. African Technology Policy Studies Network-Nairobi

Dunn, P. D. (1978). Appropriate Technology: Technology with a human face. The Macmillan Press Ltd, London

Mburugu, J. B. & Thion'go, J. M. (Eds.). (1991). *Entrepreneurship Education in Kenya: Promoting Entrepreneurship Education in Technical Training Institutes.* Nairobi: Government Printer.

Nafukho, F. M. (1993). University students need entrepreneurial skills." *Daily Nation, April 6, 1993.*

Nafukho, F. M. (1997a). Business skills essential. Daily Nation Black Board Column. *Daily Nation Inc.* Nairobi, Kenya. July 19, 1997, p.19.

Nafukho, F. M. (1997b). Attitude change vital for entrepreneurship studies. Daily Nation Black Board Column. Daily Nation Inc., Nairobi, Kenya. November 22, 1997, 16-17.

Nafukho, F. M. (1998). Entrepreneurial skills development programs for the unemployed youth in Africa: A second look. *Journal of Small Business Management, 36(*1), 100-103.

Nafukho, F. M. (2006). Let us harness our ideas to create wealth. *The East African Standard,* Interactive Column, January 4, 2006, 1.

Nafukho, F. M. (2007). *Entrepreneurship education and micro small and medium size enterprises. K*eynote paper presented at Kenyatta University during the International Conference on Micro and Small Business Enterprises, Kenyatta University, Nairobi Kenya, Organized by the Center for Entrepreneurship Education, School of Business, November 14 – 17th, 2007.

Nafukho, F. M. (2007). Is youth fund a myth or new gateway to success? Daily Nation, February 7, 2007 http://www.nationmedia.com/ dailynation/nmgcontententry.asp?category_id=25&newsid=91294

Nafukho, F. M. (2007). Is youth fund the new path to Jerusalem? http:// www.eastandard.net/hm_news/news.php?articleid=1143964550

Nafukho, F. M., (2006). How to harness peoples' creativity to create wealth. *Daily Nation,* January 6, 2006. http://www.nationmedia.com/ dailynation/nmgcontententry.asp?category_id=23&newsid=64682.

The Garden of Wisdom. (2011) Mr. Lazy – a Buddhist fol story. Retrieved November 18, 20011 from http://www.thegardenofwisdom.com/ index.html

The Holy Bible (2011) Mathew 25:14-30. New International Version> Retrieved from http://www.biblegateway.com/passage/?search=Ma tthew+25&version=NIV. On September 30, 2011.

Wambunya, T. (2005). *Luyia proverbs.* London: Luyia Publishing Company.

Weldon, C. A. (2002). Huffing and puffing through economics. Retrieved March 28, 2008 from http://ala.org/ala/booklinksbucket/ huffingpuffing.cfm